CRIME
CONTROL
AS INDUSTRY

CRIME
CONTROL
AS INDUSTRY

Towards GULAGS,
Western Style

Nils Christie

UNIVERSITY OF OSLO

Third
edition

Routledge
Taylor & Francis Group

LONDON AND NEW YORK

First published in English in 1993
Second and enlarged edition 1994
Third edition 2000
by Routledge
2 Park Square, Milton Park, Abingdon, Oxon OX14 4RN

Simultaneously published in the USA and Canada
by Routledge
270 Madison Ave, New York, NY 10016

Reprinted 2001, 2003, 2004, 2007, 2009, 2010

*Routledge is an imprint of the Taylor & Francis Group,
an informa business*

Published in Norway as Kriminalitetskontroll som industri in 1993
by Universitetsforlaget, Oslo

© 1993 Nils Christie

This edition is prepared for publishing by Scandinavian University Press, Oslo
Cover: Astrid E. Jørgensen
Printed in England by
TJ International Ltd, Padstow, Cornwall

British Library Cataloguing in Publication Data
A catalogue record for this book is available from the British Library.

Library of Congress Cataloging in Publication Data
A catalog record for this book is available from the Library of Congress.

ISBN 978-0-415-23487-0

To Ivan Illich

Preface to the third edition

This book is heavily revised.[1] The Figure in this preface tells why. It shows the number of prisoners in the USA from 1945 to 1999 per 100,000 inhabitants. The long solid line gives the numbers in State and Federal institutions, the dotted line is where jails are also included.

Prisoners in State and Federal institutions per 100,000 resident population in USA 1945–1999. And total incarceration rate 1985–1999.

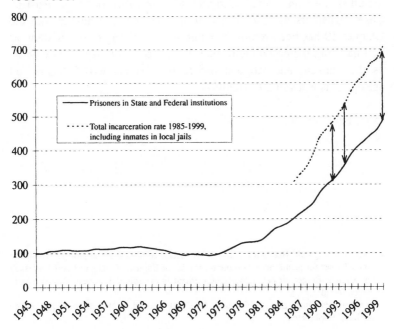

There are three arrows pointing to the curve, indicating the years for the writing and the rewriting of this book:

In 1991 – time of the first writing – the total US figures had reached the alarming level of 1,219,014 prisoners, or 482 per 100,000 inhabitants.

In 1993 – time for work on the second edition – the figures were 1,369,185 or 537 per 100,000 inhabitants. A question mark was attached to the subtitle of the first edition of this book: "Towards GULAGS, Western Style?" In the second edition, I deleted the question mark.

At the end of 1999 the USA has an estimated 1,934,532 prisoners, which equals 709 per 100,000 inhabitants. In February 2000 – when this third edition goes to print – the USA prison population hits the two million mark.[2]

The Russian development is similar, as documented in Chapters 3 and 6. What was alarming in 1991, has developed into a catastrophe at the turn of the century.

To keep track of these and other developments, I have reorganized and rewritten large parts of the book. Two completely new chapters are included, one on "Penal Geography", the other on "The Russian Case". Chapters 4, 5, 7, 8, and 9 are considerably altered, the old Chapter 10 has been removed, while the remaining chapters stand as is. I have not increased the format. In the Icelandic Sagas, they wrote as they talked, and stopped before their (imagined) listeners fell asleep. This is a valuable tradition.

Oslo, February 2000
N.C.

1 Thanks to Ragnhild Hennum for invaluable assistance in this whole process. Thanks to Anne Turner for gentle help with the intricacies of English. Thanks to Marit Hatleskog and Rigmor Berget for help and encouragement in the editorial process. And thanks to Hedda for all.
2 Los Angeles Times Service, February 16, 2000 – based on data from Justice Policy Institute, Washington.

Contents

Chapter 1

Efficiency and decency

This book is a warning against recent developments in the field of crime control. The theme is simple. Societies of the Western type face two major problems: Wealth is everywhere unequally distributed. So is access to paid work. Both problems contain potentialities for unrest. The crime control industry is suited for coping with both. This industry provides profit and work while at the same time producing control of those who otherwise might have disturbed the social process.

Compared to most other industries, the crime control industry is in a most privileged position. There is no lack of raw-material; crime seems to be in endless supply. Endless are also the demands for the service, as well as the willingness to pay for what is seen as security. And the usual industrial questions of contamination do not appear. On the contrary, this is an industry seen as cleaning up, removing unwanted elements from the social system.

Only rarely will those working in or for any industry say that now, just now, the size is about right. Now we are big enough, we are well established, we do not want any further growth. An urge for expansion is built into industrial thinking, if for no other reason than to forestall being swallowed up by competitors. The crime control industry is no exception. But this is an industry with particular advantages, providing weapons for what is often seen as a permanent war against crime. The crime control industry is like rabbits in Australia or wild mink in Norway – there are so few natural enemies around.

Belief in being at war is one strong driving force behind the development. A general adaptation to industrialized ways of thought, organization and behaviour is another. The institution of law is in a process of change. The old-fashioned symbol was Lady Justice, blindfolded, and with scales in her hand. Her task was to balance a great number of opposing values. That role is threatened. A silent revolution has taken place within the institution of law, a revolution which provides increased opportunities for growth within the control industry.

Through these developments, a situation is created where a heavy increase in the number of prisoners must be expected. But there are counter-forces in action. As will soon be documented, enormous discrepancies in prison figures exist between countries otherwise relatively similar. We are also confronted with "inexplicable" variations within the same countries over time. Prison figures may go down in periods where they, according to crime statistics, economic and material conditions, ought to have gone up, and they may go up where they for the same reasons ought to have gone down. Behind these "irregular" moves, we find ideas on what is seen as right and fair to do to other beings, ideas which counteract "rational" economic-industrial solutions. The first chapters of this book document the effects of these counter-forces.

My lesson from all this is as follows: In our present situation, so extraordinarily well suited for growth, it is particularly important to realize that the size of the prison population is a normative question. We are both free and obliged to choose. Limits to the growth of the prison industry have to be man-made. We are in a situation with an urgent need for a serious discussion on how large the system of formal control can be allowed to grow. Thoughts, values, ethics – and not industrial drive – must determine the limits of control, the question of when enough is enough. The size of the prison population is a result of decisions. We are free to choose. It is only when we are not aware of this freedom that the economic/material conditions are given free reign. Crime control is an industry. But industries have to be balanced. This book is about the drive in the prison industry, but also about the counter-forces in morality.

Nothing said here means that protection of life, body and property is of no concern in modern society. On the contrary, living in large scale societies will sometimes mean living in settings where representatives of law and order are seen as the essential guarantee for safety. Not taking this problem seriously serves no good purpose. All modern societies will have to do something about what are generally perceived as crime problems. States have to control these problems; they have to use money, people and buildings. What follows will not be a plea for a return to a stage of social life without formal control. It is a plea for reflections on limits.

Behind my warning against these developments lurks a shadow from our recent history. Studies on concentration camps and Gulags have brought us important new insights. The old questions were wrongly formulated. The problem is not: How could it happen? The problem is rather: Why does it not happen more often? And when, where and how will it happen next time?[1] Zygmunt Bauman's book *Modernity and the Holocaust* (1989) is a landmark in this thinking.

Modern systems of crime control contain certain potentialities for developing into Gulags, Western type. With the cold war brought to an end, in a situation with deep economic recession, and where the most important industrial nations have no external enemies to mobilize against, it seems not improbable that the war against the inner enemies will receive top priority according to well-established historical precedents. Gulags, Western type will not exterminate, but they have the possibility of removing from ordinary social life a major segment of potential trouble-makers for most of those persons' lives. They have the potentiality of transforming what otherwise would have been those persons' most active life-span into an existence very close to the German expression of a life not worth living. "... there is no type of nation-state in the contemporary world which is completely immune from the potentiality of being subject to totalitarian rule," says Anthony Giddens (1984, p. 309). I would like to add: The major

1 It can rightly be said: The question is not when or where the Holocaust will happen next. It is already happening. Western industrial and financial policy results each day in death and destruction in the Third World. Nonetheless, I will in this book limit my attention to the situation within the industrial world. Crime control in the west is a microcosmos. If we understand what is happening within some of these countries, we may come closer to an understanding of Third World phenomena.

dangers of crime in modern societies are not the crimes, but that the fight against them may lead societies towards totalitarian developments.

It is a deeply pessimistic analysis I here present, and as such, in contrast to what I believe is my basic attitude to much in life. It is also an analysis of particular relevance to the USA, a country I for many reasons feel close to. I have conveyed parts of my analysis to American colleagues in seminars and lectures inside and outside the USA, and I know they become unhappy. They are not necessarily disagreeing, on the contrary, but are unhappy at being seen as representatives – which they are – of a country with particular potentialities for developments like those I outline. It is of limited comfort in this situation to be assured that the chances are great that Europe may once again follow the example set by the big brother in the West.

But a warning is also an act of some optimism. A warning implies belief in possibilities for change.

The book is dedicated to Ivan Illich. His thoughts are behind so much of what is formulated here, and he also means much to me personally. Illich does not write on crime control as such, but he has seen the roots of what is now happening: the tools which create dependence, the knowledge captured by experts, the vulnerability of ordinary people when they are brought to believe that answers to their problems are in other peoples' heads and hands. What takes place within the field of industrialized crime control is the extreme manifestation of developments Ivan Illich has continually warned against. I include references to some of his major works in the list of literature, even though they are not directly referred to in the text. They are in it, nonetheless.

Some final remarks on my intentions, and on language and form:

What here follows is an attempt to create a coherent understanding based on a wide range of phenomena most often treated separately. Several chapters might have been developed into separate books, but my interest has been to present them together and thereby open up the exploring of their interrelationships. I make an attempt to help the readers to find these interrelationships themselves, without too much enforced interpretation from me. The material I present might also be given quite different interpretations than those I have in mind. That would be fine. I do not want to create closure, enclosure, but to open up new perspectives in the endless search for meaning.

Then on language and form: Sociological jargon is usually filled with latinized concepts and complicated sentence structures. It is as if the use of ordinary words and sentences might decrease the trust in arguments and reasoning. I detest that tradition. So little of the sociology I am fond of needs technical terms and ornate sentences. I write with my "favourite aunts" in mind, fantasy figures of ordinary people, sufficiently fond of me to give the text a try, but not to the extent of using terms and sentences made complicated to look scientific.

Chapter 2

The Eye of God

2.1 All alone

It is Sunday morning. The inner city of Oslo is as if deserted. The gates to the garden surrounding the University were locked when I arrived. So were the entrance door to the Institute and the door to my office. I am convinced I am the only living person in the whole complex. Nobody can see me. I am free from all sorts of control except the built-in ones.

Historically, this is a rather exceptional situation. Seen by nobody, except myself. It was not the life of my grandmothers, or of my mother, at least not completely. And the further back in the line I move, the more sure I am; they were never alone, they were always under surveillance. As a minimum: God was there. He may have been an understanding God, accepting some deviance, considering the total situation. Or He was a forgiving one. But He was always around.

So were also ordinary people.

Towards the end of the eleventh century, the Inquisition was at work in France. Some of the unbelievably detailed protocols from the interrogations are still preserved in the Vatican, and Ladurie (1978) has used them to reconstruct life in the mountain village Montaillou from 1294 to 1324. He describes the smell, the sounds and the transparency. Dwellings were not for privacy. They were not built for it, partly due to material limitations, but also because privacy was not that important a consideration. If the Almighty saw it all, why then struggle to keep the neighbours out? This merged with an ancient tradition. The very term "private" is rooted in the Latin *privare* – which is related to loss, being robbed – deprivation. I am deprived here on Sunday morning, completely alone behind the locked gates and doors of the University.

2.2 The stranger

It was in Berlin in 1903 that Georg Simmel published his famous essay on "The Stranger – Exkurs über den Fremden". To Simmel, the stranger was not the person who arrives today and walks off tomorrow. The stranger was the person who arrives today and stays on both tomorrow and maybe forever, but all the time with the potentiality to leave. Even if he does not go away, he has not quite abandoned freedom in the possibility of leaving. This he knows. So do his surroundings. He is a participant, a member, but less so than other people. The surroundings do not quite have a total grip on him.

Georg Simmel would have enjoyed *Diagram 2.2-1*.

The unbroken line which hits the roof gives the number per 1,000 inhabitants of all cases of crime investigated by the police in Norway from 1956 to 1997. This is as usual in most industrialized societies. In absolute numbers it is an increase from 26,140 to 272,651 cases. The other line – here, since they are so few, measured per 100,000 inhabitants rather than per 1,000 as in the line for all crimes – shows cases of crimes against honour, libel and slander, acts which are still seen as crimes in my country. As we observe, the trend here is in the opposite direction. Crimes against people's honour have gone down substantially during the last 35 years – in absolute figures from 1,103 to 745.

My interpretation is trivial. People are not more kind to each other or more careful in respecting other people's honour. The general explanation is simply that there is not so much to lose. Honour is not so important any more that one goes to the police when it is offended. Modern societies have an abundance of arrangements – intended and not so intended – which have as their end result that other people do

Diagram 2.2-1. All types of reported crimes investigated per 1,000 inhabitants, and slander and libel investigated per 100,000 inhabitants. Norway 1956–1997.

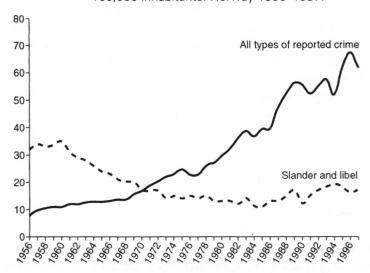

not matter to the extent they once did. Our destiny is to be alone – private – or surrounded by people we only know to a limited extent, if we know them at all. Or we are surrounded by people we know we can easily leave, or who will leave us with the situation of the stranger. In this situation, loss of honour does not become that important. No one will know us at our next station in life. But by that very token, our surroundings also lose some of their grip upon us, and the line for all registered crimes gets an extra upward push.

2.3 Where crime does not exist

One way of looking at crime is to perceive it as a sort of basic phenomenon. Certain acts are seen as inherently criminal. The extreme case is natural crime, acts so wrong that they virtually define themselves as crimes, or are at least regarded as crimes by all reasonable humans. If not seen so, these are not humans. This view is probably close to what most people intuitively feel, think, and say about serious crime. Moses came down with the rules, Kant used natural crimes as a basis for his legal thinking.

But systems where such views prevail also place certain limits on the trend towards criminalization.

The underlying mechanism is simple. Think of children. Our own children and those of others. Most children sometimes act in ways that according to the law might be called crimes. Some money may disappear from a purse. The son does not tell the truth, at least not the whole truth, as to where he spent the evening. He beats his brother. But still, we do not apply categories from penal law. We do not call the child a criminal and we do not call the acts, crimes.

Why?

It just does not feel right.

Why not?

Because we know too much. We know the context, the son was in desperate need of money, he was in love for the first time, his brother had teased him more than anybody could bear – his acts were meaningful, nothing was added by seeing them from the perspective of penal law. And the son himself; we know him so well from thousands of encounters. In that totality of knowledge a legal category is much too narrow. He took that money, but we remember all the times he generously shared his money or sweets or warmth. He hit his brother, but has more often comforted him; he lied, but is basically deeply trustworthy.

He is. But this is not necessarily true of the kid who just moved in across the street.

Acts are not, they *become*. So also with crime. Crime does not exist. Crime is created. First there are acts. Then follows a long process of giving meaning to these acts. Social distance is of particular importance. Distance increases the tendency to give certain acts the meaning of being crimes, and the persons the simplified meaning of being criminals. In other settings – family life is only one of several examples – the social conditions are of a sort which creates resistance against perceiving acts as crimes and persons as criminals.

2.4 An unlimited supply of crime

In societies with limited tendencies to perceive acts as crimes, and where most potentialities for such acts are prevented by God's eye, neighbours' attendance and situational restrictions, law can be seen as a receiver of the left-over. Law becomes here a receiver of the totality of the little that has slipped through the first line of control, and has come to the attention of authorities. In this situation, there is neither room nor need for a discussion of *selection of cases*. The judges have to take what comes before them. Re-act.[2]

But as we have seen, this is not our situation. The social system has changed into one where there are fewer restraints against perceiving even minor transgressions of laws as crimes and their actors as criminals. And then, at the same time, we are in a situation where the old defences against committing unwanted acts are gone, while new technical forms of control have been created. God and neighbours have been replaced by the mechanical efficiency of modern forms of surveillance. We live in a concrete situation with crime as a mass-phenomenon. Here anger and anxieties created from acts which also in modern societies might easily have been perceived as natural crimes become the driving force in the fight against all sorts of deplorable acts. *This new situation, with an unlimited reservoir of acts which can be defined as crimes, also creates unlimited possibilities for warfare against all sorts of unwanted acts.*

With a living tradition from the period where natural crimes were the only ones, combined with an unlimited reservoir of what can be seen as crimes in modern times, the ground has been prepared. The crime control market is waiting for its entrepreneurs.

---

2 When they punish the offender it is not their responsibility. The responsibility rests with the person who has committed what we might call "the natural crime". Such a re-active framework – in contrast to a pro-active one – gives considerable protection to those who run the system. The responsibility for what later happens is seen as resting solidly on the person who commits the crime. She/he acts, and the authorities are forced to re-act. The law-breaker starts it all; authorities only restore the balance.

Chapter 3

Penal geography

3.1 Maps of pain

In this chapter, maps will be used to give a visual picture of the use of imprisonment in Europe and America. Other parts of the globe ought to have been included. I have the figures, but lack adequate knowledge of the social settings to give them sufficient meaning in the chapters that follow. Figures without meaning represent noise in a social analysis. Many of the figures I use stem from Roy Wamsley's (1999) extremely useful study. Some of them are provided through my own contacts in the countries I cover.

The amount of punishment used by the legal system in any country can be measured in several ways. I will mostly present data on imprisonment. Next to execution, imprisonment is the strongest punitive measure at the disposal of any state. All of us are under some sort of restraint, forced to work to survive, forced to submit to superiors, captured in social classes or class-rooms, tied into various forms of formal or informal networks. But except for Capital Punishment and physical torture – measures put to limited use in most of the countries discussed in this book – nothing is so total in constraints, in degradation, and in its display of power, as is the prison.

As a measure, I will mostly use a relative figure, which is the daily number of prisoners per 100,000 inhabitants. This is not a precise indicator, but the best we can find when we are to compare nations. Steenhuis and collaborators (1983) are critical of this use. A low relative figure, they argue, might be the result of many prisoners with short sentences, or just a few prisoners sentenced for life. I am not fully convinced. Independently of the distribution between short and long sentences, it seems reasonable to say that a country with 500 prisoners per 100,000 inhabitants is one that uses measures of intended pain more than a society with 50 prisoners per 100,000 inhabitants.[1]

3.2 Europe – West

Map 3.2-1 gives a picture of the general situation. Two elements are clearly visible.

First, we can observe great variations in prison figures, even between neighbours as close as those within Western Europe. Iceland is at the bottom with 40 prisoners per 100,000 of the population, while Portugal is at the very top with 145.

A second feature of the map, a rather surprising one, is the company some of these countries end up in. The three top-raters are Portugal with its 145 prisoners, the United Kingdom with 125, and then Spain with 110 prisoners per 100,000.

At the more ordinary Central European level we find Austria, Belgium, France, Germany and the Netherlands, all with figures in the range between 95 and 80 per 100,000.

At the very bottom, we find the Scandinavian countries and also Ireland and Greece. That the Scandinavians have similarities, is not so surprising, with the exception of Finland which I will comment on in Chapter 4.4. But Ireland? The difference between Ireland and the

---

1 The number of new prison intakes is sometimes suggested as an indicator (e.g. Pease, 1994). This, however, raises the problem of defining what a new intake is. To be brought into the police station, is that an intake? A stay in a waiting cell for 4, 8 or 24 hours, is that to be counted? Or is it only imprisonment according to orders by a judge? In some jurisdictions, such decisions have to take place within 24 hours. In others, the police can wait for several weeks or months before a person is brought before a judge and his incarceration is counted as incarceration. In some jurisdictions a person moved from custody to serving a sentence is counted as a new intake. For these reasons, I keep to the number of incarcerated persons.

Map 3.2-1. EUROPE – WEST
(Greenland 220)

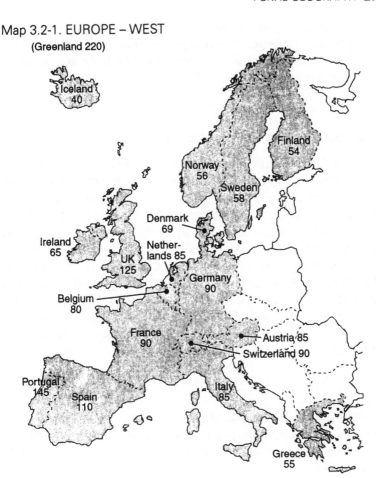

United Kingdom is remarkable. Ireland has 65 prisoners per 100,000 of the population and the United Kingdom has 125, close to the double. Are they in other respects also that different? And the United Kingdom, compared to Scandinavia? So little water between the United Kingdom and Scandinavia, and so close in culture, but so different in the use of the intended delivery of pain?

It has not always been like this. Once, the United Kingdom belonged to the low incarcerators. This was before World War I. Winston Churchill was in command of the Home Office, he was indignant at finding so many poor people in prison, he had power to act, and brought down the prison figures to below 30 per 100,000 inhabitants. It is the new Britain that brought them up to 125. In the first edition of this book, the figure was 90.

3.3 Europe – Central and East

Map 3.3-1 illustrates the present situation. As we can see, Russia is the Big Power in Europe – when it comes to incarceration. The official figure is 685 prisoners per 100,000. That is more than ten times the Scandinavian level, and five times the one for the United Kingdom. And Russia is clearly the trend-setter for countries close to her. Belarus has 505, then follows Ukraine with 415, and, surprisingly, the Baltic states, with 410 in Latvia, 355 in Lithuania and 320 in Estonia. Moldavia and Rumania are at 260 and 200 respectively, the Czech Republic at 215, and Poland and Georgia at 145, while Slovakia and Bulgaria have 140 and Hungary 135. Little Slovenia has established itself at the same level as Iceland, with 40 prisoners per 100,000.

***

Given the dominant position of Russia, it is necessary to look in some detail at what is happening there. The development since World War II, or the great patriotic war as the Russians call it, is illustrated in *Table 3.3-1*.

This table has not been easy to establish. My first visit to Russia was in 1967. At that time, the statistics on crimes and punishments were deep secrets. And this secrecy continued during all the years up to 1989. But slowly the state softened and the figures leaked out. I am rather proud of one particular method I used to obtain the figures. I call it "the humming-method". Colleagues in the old USSR could not tell me how many prisoners they had. But these colleagues had faces, and they produced sounds. I remember particularly a joint Scandinavian–USSR research meeting in Sweden in 1989. Here I presented several preliminary figures I had gathered on the USSR prison population, and asked for a sort of reaction. The answers came – in body language. Extreme

Map 3.3-1. EUROPE – CENTRAL AND EAST

Russian
Federation
685

Estonia 320
Latvia 410
Lithuania 355
Belorus
505
Poland
145
Czech Rep.
215
Slovakia
140
Ukraine
415
Moldavia
260
Hungary
135
Slovenia
40
Rumania
200
Georgia
145
Bulgaria
140
Turkey
95

figures as those for 1979 of 660 per 100,000 inhabitants were received with irritation. A suggestion of 214 per 100,000 was received with polite smiles indicating my naiveté. The figure 353 – which at that time had become my favourite estimate – was received with satisfied silence. Today, the prison figures are not secret any more.

As we observe from the table, the prison population of 1950 is close to being unbelievably high. 1400 per 100,000, or 1.4 percent of the total

Table 3.3-1. Prisoners per 100,000 inhabitants in USSR/Russia
1950-1999

Year	Prisoners per 100,000 inhabitants
1950	1400
1979	660
1989	353
1993	573
1994	611
1995	685
1996	704
1998	685
1999	685

population, babies and old folks included, were at that time in prisons or GULAGS.[2]

In 1979, a former prosecutor in the USSR estimated their prison figures for that year to be 660 per 100,000. These were given in a presentation to the American Society of Criminology. Then followed 1989 with Glasnost and Gorbachev and all that, and the prison figures went down to 353. But as we know, and also see from our table, Glasnost was only an interval, and the figures have from that time moved only one way. The relative number of prisoners has nearly doubled since 1989. What is now Russia has one million prisoners, or 685 per 100,000 of the population. If we include people involuntarily detained in certain "treatment-institutions", the relative figures end up slightly above 700 per 100,000 (Abramkin, personal communication, summer 1999). Now the increase seems to have come to a stop. The numbers have not risen in the last two or three years. An amnesty given 70,000 prisoners during the spring of 1999 has not led to a decrease compared with the preceding years, but has helped to stabilise the situation.

2 This figure is based on figures from the Academy of Science in Moscow. The Academy was asked in 1989 by Mr. Gorbachev to investigate the secret archives of the Ministry of the Interior. Several groups of historians were established, directed by Viktor N. Semskov. Semskov has published a preliminary report, to me only available indirectly (Bech 1992). The major finding is that the GULAGS reached their maximum in 1950 with 2.5 million prisoners. Based on the population in the USSR at that time, this equals 1423 prisoners per 100,000 inhabitants.

The major types of penal institutions in Russia are prisons and colonies. Prisons are mostly for those prisoners awaiting trial, SIZO-prisoners as they are called. Their numbers are steadily increasing, from 150,000 in 1990, 251,000 in 1998 and 269,000 in 1999.[3] These prisoners live under awful conditions. After sentencing, prisoners are transferred to what are now called "colonies", previously known as GULAGS.[4] Here conditions are generally better.

There is much more to say about Russia. So much, that we will need the whole of Chapter 6 for that purpose. But already now one conclusion is clear: Russia is the great incarcerator of Europe.

3.4 America – North

For North America, we do not need any map as our point of departure. It is enough with two figures. They are:

129

and

709

The first is the number of prisoners in Canada per 100,000 inhabitants. The second is the number of prisoners in the USA. Two countries, so close, joint border, same language for the most part, same type of media, same heritage, same economic system, to some extent common thoughts about money. But with an administrative structure in Canada close to the British. And also with more of a social safety-net still in place.

An overview of the prison situation in the USA is presented in *Table 3.4-1*. In the first row we find the official figures for 1998. It shows figures for the three major types of prisons. In Federal and State institutions, the more severe sentences are served. As we can see from the table, these are where the bulk of the prisoners are. Roughly one-third of the inmates serve their time in jails – institutions run by local

---

3 Vedomosti Uglovno-Ispravitelnoy Sistemi Rossi (The Gazette of the Penal-Executive System of the Russian Ministry of Justice. 1998, Special Issue.)
4 Named after Glanoye Upravlenie Lagerei – the Central Administration of Camps.

Table 3.4-1. Number of persons in prisons and jails in the USA 1998,[1] and estimated[2] numbers for 1999. Total and per 100,000.

	1998	Estimated addition	1999 (Estimated)
Federal and state prisons	1,232,900	80,139	1,313,039
Jails	592,462	29,031	621,493
Total	1,825,362	109,170	1,934,532
Per 100,000 total population	672		709[3]

1 Prisoners in State and Federal prisons on December 31 and inmates in local jails on June 30 (from Bureau of Justice Statistics, Bulletin, "Prisoners in 1998"). The numbers exclude persons supervised outside of a prison or jail facility.
2 Estimate is based on the average annual increase 1990-98. For prisoners in State and Federal prisons the average annual increase is 6.5%. For inmates in local jails the average annual increase is 4.9% (from Bureau of Justice Statistics, Bulletin, "Prisoners in 1998", p. 2).
3 Based on an estimated population of 273 million for midyear 1999.

authorities. But this does not necessarily mean that they serve only short sentences. Due to the lack of space in Federal and State prisons, the jails have been forced to receive prisoners that strictly belong to the Federal and State systems.

The general impression given by the table is the enormity of the figures. Let us first look at the figures in the first row. These are the last available official ones. We find here a total prison population for 1998 of 1.8 million inmates, or 672 per 100,000 inhabitants. But these figures are already outdated, the growth is so fast. So in the middle row we have estimated the number of new prisoners from 1998 to 1999, using the same figures for annual growth as were provided for 1990 to 1998. Calculated as we do it here, we estimated that the USA on the last day of this century will have more than 1.9 million prisoners, or 709 per 100,000 of the population, at this time.

Close to all of these are adults. If we compare the 1.9 million prisoners with the number of adults in the population, we find, as illustrated in *Table 3.4-2*, that 956 per 100,000 of the adult population are under this sort of control.

Table 3.4-2. Number of persons in prisons and jails in the USA 1998,[1] and estimated numbers for 1999. Total and per 100,000 adults.[2]

	1998	1999
Total number of persons in prisons and jails	1,825,362	1,934,532
Per 100,000 adults	911[3]	956[4]

1 Prisoners in State and Federal prisons on December 31 and inmates in local jails on June 30 (from Bureau of Justice Statistics, Bulletin, "Prisoners in 1998"). The numbers exclude persons supervised outside of a prison or jail facility.
2 Persons 18 years and above.
3 1 July there were 200.4 million US residents 18 years and above.
4 1 May there were 202.3 million US residents 18 years and above.

The United States also keeps good statistics on persons under the control of penal law outside the prisons. This makes it possible to construct *Table 3.4-3*. Here we find three categories. At the top is repeated the total number of prisoners from *Table 3.4-1*. The second line gives the number supervised by prison personnel, but outside of the ordinary prisons or jails. Then, in the third line, come persons on probation and parole. The first figure on probation and parole is from 1 January 1998, and the estimated one from 1999. At the bottom of the table, we find the total population under penal control in absolute figures, and per 100,000 of that population.

Table 3.4-3. Number of persons under control of the penal law system in the USA 1998, and estimated number for 1999.

	1998	1999
Prisoners	1,825,362	1,934,532
Supervised outside prisons or jails	140,217	146,187
Probation and parole, beginning of year[1]	3,946,921	4,107,584[2]
Total population under penal control	5,912,500	6,188,303
Per 100,000 of population	2,187	2,267[3]

1 Department of Justice (1998).
2 Based on a 3% growth among probationers and 1.3% among parolees – the same as the previous year. The annual growth for both since 1990 was 3% – which would have given us a slightly higher estimate (18,725 persons).
3 Based on a population of 273 million.

Table 3.4-4. Number of persons under control of the penal law
system in the USA 1998, and estimated number for
1999. Adults, and adults in age 18-44.

	1998	1999
Total population under penal control	5,912,500	6,188,303
Per 100,000 adults	2,950[1]	3,059[2]
Per 100,000 adults in age 18–44[3]	4,623[4]	4,835[5]

1 1 July 1998 there were 200.4 million US residents 18 years and above.
2 1 May 1999 there were 202.3 million US residents 18 years and above.
3 The numbers are based on 85% of the persons under penal control being adults in age 18-44 years. For 1998
   this gives 5,025,625 persons under control and for 1999, 5,260,058 persons under control.
4 1 July 1998 there were 108.7 million US residents 18-44 years.
5 1 May 1999 there were 108.8 million US residents 18-44 years.

In total, an estimated 6.2 million US citizens are under the control of
the penal law system. This means, in 1999, 2267 persons per 100,000
inhabitants – or 2.3% of the total population.

Most of those controlled by the penal system are relatively young
people. Our estimate is that 87% of all prisoners in Federal and State
prisons are 44 years or younger.[5] In jails, 92% are that young.
Probationers might be slightly older, so, to be on the safe side, let us
suppose that no more than 85% of the total population under penal
control are between 18 and 44 years old. Compared to the population
in that age group, we see from *Table 3.4-4* that this gives us 4835 per
100,000 in 1999. In other words, close to 5% of the population from
18 to 44 are under the control of the penal law system.

If we also split these figures according to sex, the situation becomes
even more extreme for the males. Roughly 90% of the prisoners are
males. So are also 80% of the probationers and 89% of the parolees.
The figures are presented in *Table 3.4-5*. We see from this table that an
estimated number of 5,221,484 of all US males are under the control
of the penal system in 1999. Or simply: of the total of 6.2 million
persons under penal control, 5.2 million are males, which means 3,923

5 Based on figures from the US Department of Justice, April 1996, *Table 1.11*, combined with the Resident Population Estimate, 1 April, 1990 to 1 May, 1999. The
   females are probably slightly older, and this might also be the case for those on probation and parole.

Table 3.4-5. Estimated number of males in the US population controlled by the penal system 1999. Total and per
100,000.

	1999
90% of 2,080,719 prisoners and persons supervised outside prisons[1]	1,872,647
80% of 3,410,135 probationers[2]	2,728,108
89% of 697,449 parolees[3]	620,729
Total number of males	5,221,484
Controlled males per 100,000 males in the population[4]	3,923

1 This is a conservative estimate. Prisoners in State and Federal prisons on 31 December and inmates in local
jails on 30 June.
2 Source: Department of Justice (16 August 1998).
3 Source as in note 2.
4 Population base, 133.1 million for 1 May 1999 (latest available).

males per 100,000 are controlled by the penal system. Nearly all these
are adults. If we use the adult population as our base – as in *Table
3.4-6* – we find that 5,377 per 100,000 of the adult population are
under such control. If we concentrate on the younger half of the male
population, we find that 8,159 per 100,000 – more than 8% – are under
the control of the penal apparatus.

The conclusion is inevitable: The USA is a state where an exceptionally large part of the population is living under the direct control of the
penal law system. This is about equal to Russia when we compare
prison populations, but when we also include probation and parole, the

Table 3.4-6. Estimated number of males in the US population controlled by the penal system, 1999. Adults, and adults
in age 18-44.

	1999
Total number of controlled males	5,221,484
Controlled males per 100,000 adult males[1]	5,377
Controlled males per 100,000 males in age 18-44[2]	8,159

1 1 May 1999 there were 97.1 million males 18 years and above.
2 1 May 1999 there were 54.4 million males in age 18-44 years. The numbers are based on 85% of the males
under penal control being adults in age 18-44 years. For 1999 this gives 4,438,261 males (18-44) under penal
control.

USA has a much larger part of its population under the control of the penal system than any other industrialized state in Europe or America.

3.5 America – Central and South

The situation in Central and South America is illustrated in *Map 3.5-1* and *Map 3.5-2*. We find Chile at the top with 375 prisoners per 100,000. Panama follows with 270, then comes Honduras (160), Costa Rica (155), and El Salvador (150). Seen from the bottom, we find Paraguay with 60 per 100,000, Guatemala with 65, Bolivia with 70 and Nicaragua with 80 per 100,000 inhabitants.

Warning bells ought to sound in the interpretation of these figures. Some of these nations have good systems for counting their prisoners. It might, therefore, look as if they have more prisoners than others. Some, however, do not include military arrests, some do not count police arrests, even when prisoners might spend years in conditions which defy description. I have visited one such place. It was in the

Map 3.5-1. CENTRAL AMERICA

Map 3.5-2. SOUTH AMERICA

centre of a glittering capital. Next to the prison was an international hotel, eight or ten floors high – hotels need room for their spacious hallways, restaurants, suites, double and single rooms, and equipment for the air-conditioning necessary to survive in the tropics. The guests in the hotel would probably identify the little nearby building simply as a police station. The prison in the backyard of the station did not occupy much space. Four or five rooms for the prisoners, 300 people in one of them, packed together, no air-conditioning, no external area for exercising. Some prisoners claimed to have stayed there for years.

A deep analysis of these figures from Central and South America is outside my competence. I present them here primarily to create a background for a more thorough understanding of the situation in North America. In this total picture, the situation in the USA becomes even more accentuated. It is not characteristic of America as a whole to have extremely high prison figures. The USA is an extremely deviant case, surrounded as it is by Canada and Mexico, culturally and economically two vastly different countries, but both with prison populations below 130 per 100,000 inhabitants.

3.6 The importance of thought patterns

Thought patterns and general theories are not impractical symbols in brains or books. They clear the way for action. The belief in prison populations as indicators of crime, and the resistance this belief shows to the facts are in harmony with the old perspectives based on natural law, and with reactive thinking. If the criminal starts it and all the authorities can do is react, then, naturally, the volume of prisoners is caused by crime and reflects the crime situation. It becomes destiny, not choice.

But modern societies have at their disposal an unlimited reservoir of acts which can be defined as crimes. And we have now seen that they make very different uses of this reservoir; at least they differ in their use of one of the most important forms of delivery of pain: imprisonment. Having reached this conclusion, we are able to move on to new questions: If the volume of crime does not explain the volume of imprisonment, how can that volume then be explained? How can we explain the enormous variations we have found, over time and between societies?

I will make an attempt in two stages. This is because two problems are equally fascinating. What these societies have in common is that – with important variations – they are highly industrialized. How then are they so different with regard to the use of imprisonment?

The first problem, therefore, is: Why do we find some of these societies making such a limited use of imprisonment? What are the social mechanisms behind a low prison population?

And then to the second problem: What are the mechanisms behind the high-raters? Why do we find societies in that same family of industrialized nations with more than ten times as many prisoners as those with the smallest prison populations?

Chapters 4 and 5 discuss some general mechanisms behind the low versus the high penalisers. But this is no more than a beginning. To come closer to an understanding of the mechanisms behind the extraordinarily high numbers of prisoners, Chapter 6 contains a case study from Russia, while the USA gets most of our attention from Chapter 7 onwards.

Chapter 4

Why are there so few prisoners?

4.1 Encounters in the mountains

Every year, just after Christmas, an unusual meeting takes place somewhere in the Norwegian mountains. By now it has become a sort of tradition, after having gone on for twenty years. The meeting is held in a hotel of quite high standing, with two hundred people participating for three days and two nights.

Five groups are there.

First: Official operators of the penal law system – prison directors, guards, doctors, social workers, probation officers, prison teachers, judges, police.

Second: Politicians – members of the Storting (the Legislative Assembly), sometimes Ministers, always advisers of some sort, and local politicians.

Third: The "liberal opposition" – lay people interested in criminal policy, students, defence lawyers, university teachers.

Fourth: People from the media.

Fifth: Prisoners, often people still serving sentences, but on leave for these days. Some arrive in cars from their prisons and in the company of staff. Others are released and arrive by ordinary bus. Not everyone is given leave of absence from prison to participate. Inmates regarded as very likely to escape are not let out. But there are often participants serving sentences for serious crimes: murder, drugs, armed robbery, espionage. During late evenings and nights one can see – if one happens to know who is who – prisoners, prison directors, guards, policemen and representatives of the liberal opposition in heated discussions on penal policy in general and on prison conditions in particular. But they can also be found in relaxed and peaceful talks on the prospects for the next day's cross-country skiing.[1]

An important effect of these meetings is to include prisoners in the joint moral community of the decision-makers.

But then comes the next question: why do the authorities participate in these encounters in the mountains?

Some explanations are close at hand. It is pleasant up there, a good escape from prison or police service. But that is not enough. The stay means trouble as well. The authorities receive lots of criticism. The heated debates, personal confrontations – and then the broad coverage in the mass media.

Much more important than the pleasures of mountain-life is probably the phenomenon of membership in a joint moral community. Norway is a small country. Those with the responsibility for running the formal system of crime control cannot avoid knowing each other, or at least *of* each other. They cannot escape their critics, and the critics cannot escape those with responsibility. We are forced into some degree of proximity. The situation does not lend itself to complete distortion. One may have strong feelings of animosity, but often with some doubts somewhere. Maybe the other party has a point. A peculiar feature is that most of the officials are graduates in law. They are old

1 The meetings are arranged by the KROM, an organization for crime reform. They have gone on for 30 years, largely owing to the initiative and energy of Thomas Mathiesen (1974, 1990). For most of the period, Mathiesen was the chairman. Mathiesen has particularly emphasized the need for keeping such an organization on a middle course, to keep a distance from both the most radical political movements and the establishment. Central in this attempt has been the acceptance of "the unfinished" as a valuable condition.

students of their even older critics. Pictures of monsters do not thrive under such conditions.

But this is too idyllic a description. The participants are a select sample. Some upholders of stern law and strict order would not dream of participating up there in the mountains. But a sufficient number from all sections are there to create communication. A sufficient number are there to leak into the system a fundamental doubt as to the productivity of more prisons, as well as some doubts about the usefulness of the trend in Europe in general and in the United States in particular.

This is not limited to the mountains. It also happens within the universities, where practitioners are often invited. And it happens within the framework of the Scandinavian Research Council for Criminology, which regularly arranges joint seminars for practitioners and researchers in various areas.

A general effect of all these meeting places has probably been to establish some kind of informal minimum standard for what is considered decent in the name of punishment, and valid for *all* human beings. Why the standards are as they are, is close to impossible to explain. I will make an attempt in Chapter 13 on Crime Control as Culture. But concerning their validity for all people, let me suggest here, as a minimum, that this has something to do with imaginative power, the capacity to see oneself in the other person's situation. In the contrasting situation, with the offender seen as another breed, a non-person, a thing, there are no limits to possible atrocities. Cohen (1992, p. 12) describes one type of justification of torture used in modern Israel:

> ... and after all, they don't really feel it, look at the violence they inflict on each other.

In public debates one often hears:
> It hurts the better situated more to be in prison.

Identification makes general standards valid for all, and functions thereby as a prevention of more extreme measures. It could have been me, found guilty, brought to prison. Identification creates the very situation Rawls (1973) constructs as an instrument to create just solutions to various conflicts. It is a situation where the decision-makers do not know which party they belong to in a conflict. Coming close to the culprits has much the same effect. It invites all sorts of inhibitions. Mentally, the judge acts, in the words of Rawls, under the veil of ignorance. He is brought close to the culprit. He might have been him. He has to decide with care.

Jessica Mitford (1974, p. 13) quotes *The New Yorker's* Talk of the Town column after the Attica uprising:

> ... millions of Americans were brought face to face with convicted criminals for the first time. Most of us were wholly unprepared for what we saw ... The crowd we saw on television was not a mob but a purposeful gathering, and the men we saw were not brutalised, although they may have suffered brutality – they were unmistakably whole men ... acting with dignity.

From the tragedy of Attica, let me again turn to Norway, to the trivialities of Norway.

4.2 Waiting for pain

For a period, we had a great lack of space in our prisons. The solution to this crisis situation was obvious. We let those sentenced wait. In 1990 we had 2,500 persons in prisons. But we had 4,500 on waiting lists. We lined them up and let them wait for admission.

Authorities were embarrassed. Waiting lists for kindergartens, waiting lists for hospitals, waiting lists for home nurses. And then waiting lists for the reception of pain. It could not be right.

I understood the uneasiness among the authorities, particularly when I tried to explain this arrangement in England or in the United States. It was as if citizens in those countries could not believe their ears. Waiting lists for imprisonment? It sounds somehow out of style, a dissonance, like a piece of hard rock in the middle of Debussy.

Why?

The uneasiness was because the arrangement was out of harmony with the current stereotypes, both of prisoners and of the functions of prisons. We all know the basic rules in games of cops and robbers. The police have to catch the robbers, throw them into prison, and keep them there. It is a tough and dangerous job. If the bad guys get a chance, they escape. This was the game of childhood. It is the game in the media, a reality according to the script. The criminal is arrested, detained while awaiting trial, and then sent straight to prison to serve his sentence.

And it is a true description, in some severe cases. But most cases are not. So, here comes the dissonance. Most sentenced people are people, ordinary people, not a special breed, not bandits. They are to blame for something, but they are not wild animals. They can wait, we all can. The drama is gone.

The queue is out of harmony with the stereotypes.[2] Recognising the queue is to recognise that those lined up there are not dangerous, are not monsters. They go to prison – eventually – for other purposes than the protection of the public. This forces us to reflect. That is why this arrangement is a good one. But the arrangement is also bad – for those in the queue. It is difficult to plan the future when on the waiting list. And people there are unhappy, knowing pain will come. Some remain passive, in their dwellings, as if in prison already. According to Fridhov (1988), those with former prison experience worry most about the coming stay in prison, they know what to expect. First-timers take it easier, they do not know.

Today, in 1999, the waiting list is gone. But of course, some are still waiting. It is a smaller queue, that is the major difference. But the basic situation is the same. Sentenced people get their letters with instructions as to when and where to serve their sentences, pack their

---

2 Waiting for trial is quite another matter. Here the villain is supposed to be under control, and the game goes on according to the script, not contrary to it. Only people interested in civil liberties sometimes mention that some of those waiting in this line might actually happen to be not guilty.

tooth-brushes and meet in front of the prison at the said time. This is as it ought to be in a civil society.

True, but not quite. Not all appear. Those serving in major prisons, that is those with long sentences, most of these arrive at the right time. So do people sentenced for drunken driving. But those more on the fringe of ordinary society, heavy drinkers, heavy drug-users, with no permanent address or living in hostels, do not follow these rules. "We have to overbook, just as the airlines do," says prison inspector Alf Bjarne Olsen. "We have two empty cells next Monday, and have asked five people to come. If they all appear, we send three of them to other prisons." This is a general trend across the country, except in the work-colony of Vestre Slidre where 95% arrive at the said time. Inspector Øyvind Kjeldsberg has this explanation: "The police have a talk with all who have to serve. They tell the police when it is best for them to serve the sentence, and we avoid a great number of problems."[3]

4.3 The good old days – they were terrible

But Scandinavian figures have also fluctuated. Norway might serve as an illustration. *Diagram 4.3-1* gives the prison figures per 100,000 inhabitants for Norway from 1814, the year we got our Constitution, up to the present. The diagram has the form of a huge mountain, with its peak firmly placed in the middle of the last century, followed by a low and relatively stable prison population throughout this century.

The increase in the prison population from 1814 is not impossible to explain. Leaving the seventeen hundreds behind, also meant abandoning a large amount of capital punishment as well as flogging, branding a thief-mark on the forehead, cutting off fingers and other mutilations. The rate of exchange prescribed for the transition from physical torment to loss of liberty was set out in an Act of 15 October 1815:

> Instead of losing a hand, imprisonment for ten years; instead of piercing the hand and rending it, imprisonment for two years; and instead of piercing the hand, imprisonment for one year.

3 Aftenposten, 21 August, 1999, p. 2.

Diagram 4.3-1. Prisoners per 100,000 inhabitants in Norway
1814–1998

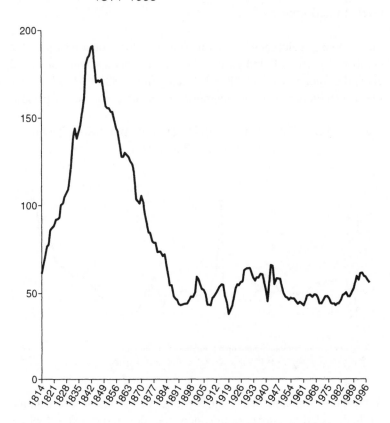

But this transition created new problems. First and foremost it caused
increased pressure on the prison system. From being one among many
forms of punishment, imprisonment now became the main response to
crime. Penitentiaries and other penal institutions became full to burst-
ing point. From 1814 to 1843, the daily number of prisoners in
Norway went up from 550 to 2,325. This represented an increase from
61 to 191 per 100,000 of the population, or a trebling in the course of
thirty years. But again something happened. A long series of amend-
ments to the penal code from 1842 to the turn of the century all tended
in the direction of shortening the periods of imprisonment, or of avoid-
ing imprisonment altogether. From the peak recorded for imprison-

ment in 1843, it took about 42 years to return to the level of 1814. Throughout this century, Norway has more or less maintained this level of imprisonment.

This whole development seems to bear no close relationship to the number of persons found guilty of crime in Norway. *Diagram 4.3-2* gives the figures per 100,000 inhabitants from 1835 to 1997. As we see if we compare the two diagrams, the relative number of persons

Diagram 4.3-2. Persons found guilty of crime per 100,000 inhabitants in Norway 1835–1997

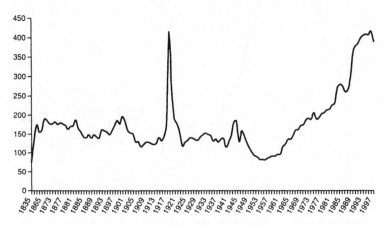

found guilty remains stable during most of the nineteenth century, while the relative number of prisoners goes down to one-fourth of the peak level in 1843. The great increase in the number of people found guilty of crime does not start until 1960. But this does not influence the prison figures.

***

Prison figures may be seen as indicators of the crime situation in a country. The criminal started it, the judiciary reacts. An increase in imprisonment is seen as indicating that crime has increased, while a downward trend indicates that the crime situation has changed for the better. Or, at the same historical point in time, societies with a high level of punishment are seen as having a high level of crime, while those with low levels are probably peaceful ponds in a turbulent world. This is the traditional way of interpreting prison figures.

But this interpretation is not in harmony with the perspective presented in Chapter 2, nor is it in harmony with the geographical distribution of prisoners. We have pointed to a situation with an unlimited reservoir of acts which can be defined as crimes. This being the case, an alternative interpretation of prison figures in the map is to see them as the end product of a myriad of influences: type of social structure, distance between people, revolutions or political upheavals, type of legal apparatus, economic interest or industrial drive. What at any particular point in time is seen as crime will certainly also play some part. It is one force, one among many. But to look at prison figures as indicators of the crime situation in a country, is much too narrow a perspective.

Let us, with this in mind, turn to Finland.

4.4 Political identification

Finland was, for a long period, the land of incarceration among the Nordic countries. *Diagram 4.4-1* gives the general picture. Three trends are visible.

First, the initial *similarity* in the developments up till 1918. But then comes the *deviation*. In 1918, the Finnish figures suddenly jump to 250 prisoners per 100,000 inhabitants. Later they fluctuate for a long time around 200 prisoners per 100,000 inhabitants, while compared with Finland the prison populations in the other Nordic countries are stabilised at quite a modest level between 50 and 100 per 100,000 inhabitants.

The third development is the recent decline in the Finnish figures, illustrated in *Diagram 4.4-2*. Here is shown the development from 1975 to 1998. From being at the top in the use of imprisonment – even according to general European standards – it is now close to the bottom.

Diagram 4.4-1. Prisoners per 100,000 inhabitants in Scandinavia
1886–1998[1]

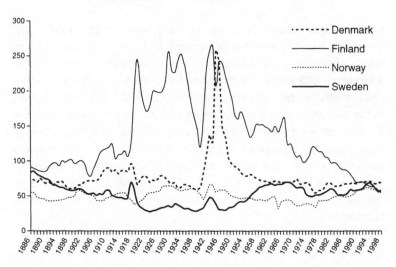

1 Figures for the imprisoned collaborators with the Germans after the Second World War are omitted for Norway. The Finnish figures do not extend further back than 1886. This was just before the deportations to Siberia came to a halt. Altogether 3236 Finnish prisoners were deported during the period 1826-1888. Figures for Norway are a bit too low in the beginning, since persons sentenced to work in the fisheries in the far North (or females working in the households up there) are not included. The Swedish figures are too low, since some administrative decisions are not included.

Seen from a national-political perspective, these three stages are rather paradoxical. From 1809, Finland was a part of Russia, but her penal policy was Nordic. From 1919, she gained her independence, but left the Nordic family and became much more punitive. But then, in the last stage, she has surpassed all Nordic countries in limiting the use of imprisonment.

We can gain some clues on this by looking more closely at history. I shall focus on the development from 1918. The dramatic increase from that year is the most simple to explain. 1918 was the year of the war of independence, followed by an unbelievably fierce civil war. Eight thousand on the losing side in that civil war were executed immediately afterwards, and an additional 100,000 perished in prison camps. This

Diagram 4.4-2. Prisoners per 100,000 inhabitants in Finland
1975–1998

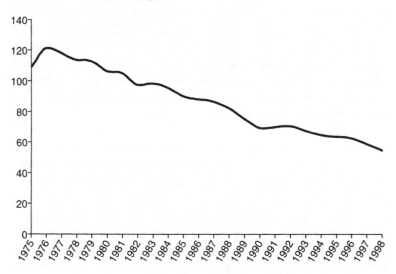

major cleavage in the population remained all the way up to the internal unity created by the two fierce wars against the USSR, first in 1939-40, and then from 1941 to 1944. Finland grew accustomed to a level of pain and suffering far beyond the usual Nordic levels.

K.J. Lång was for many years the director general of the prison system in Finland. He harbours no illusions regarding the reasons for the high prison figures (Lång 1989, pp. 83–84, in my translation):

> ... the number of prisoners has very little to do with crime. The number of prisoners is rather caused by the general situation of confidence in society and of the political equilibrium. The political turbulence during three wars, the right-wing movements of the 1930s and the criminalized communist movement (of that time), have all led to a greater use of imprisonment in Finland than in any other Nordic country. ... The legislation has meant that we got accustomed to a high punitive level with long sentences for the various crimes. ... Finland had throughout the 1970s three times as many prisoners as Norway. Not because Finland put three times as many persons in prison, but because each prisoner was kept in prison about three times as long in Finland as in Norway.

But then comes the question of the decline. What is behind the recent dramatic decrease in the use of imprisonment in Finland? One reason for the decline might be that the reasons for the high level are gone. But this is not necessarily sufficient as an explanation. Social conditions tend to remain, out of tradition and vested interests. What is, is, because it is. But something happened in Finland. Patrik Tørnudd (1991) describes it. He points to a unique combination of historical antecedents, ideological constellations, and also of hard work by a number of dedicated individuals.

First of all, according to Tørnudd, it is a question of perceiving a problem as a problem. To do so, it is necessary to become aware of the fact that Finland's prisoner rate was exceptionally high. It is also necessary to understand that this was not caused by an unusual crime profile in Finland. And lastly, it is necessary to reject any attempt to see the high number of prisoners as something to be proud of e.g. as indicators of the determination and toughness of the criminal justice system or of its readiness to spend its resources on prolonged rehabilitation efforts and on the protection of the public.

According to Tørnudd, professional criminologists provided the necessary data. They documented that Finland was out of line with the rest of the Nordic countries in size of its prison population, and they refuted the popular explanation for this – that crime in Finland was very different from crime in the other Nordic countries. But this would not have been sufficient to bring down the prison population. Not only were the experts providing essential information, they were also in the position to change conditions. Tørnudd writes (p. 5–6):

> ... the Nordic countries can generally be characterised as fairly expert-oriented, and Finland has been said to be the most expert-oriented among the Scandinavian countries. Certainly it is true that crime control never has been a central political issue in election campaigns in Finland.
> ...
> But the fact that it became possible to carry out a large number of reforms aimed at reducing the level of punishment was ultimately dependent on the fact that the small group of experts who were in charge of reform planning or who worked as crime control experts in research institutes and universities shared an almost unanimous conviction that Finland's internationally

high prisoner rate was a disgrace and that it would be possible to reduce significantly the number and length of prison sentences without serious repercussions on the crime situation.

Tørnudd concludes (p. 13):

> The decisive factor in Finland was the attitudinal readiness of the civil servants, the judiciary and the prison authorities to use all available means in order to bring down the number of prisoners. Through the efforts of a group of key individuals it had become possible to define Finland's prisoner rate as a problem and that problem conception in turn produced a number of activities, ranging from law reforms to low-level day-to-day decisions, which all contributed to the end result.

But why should the Finns after World War II consider their prison figures abnormal? They were not, if they looked towards the USSR. But that was exactly where the Finns did not want to look. Finland's penal history illustrates that prison figures are not created by crime, but by cultural/political decisions. They are based on decisions on what sort of society we want to be a part of.

Finland is to Scandinavians half way to Russia. To Russians it must be like being at home. Arriving at Helsinki by train from St. Petersburg – it takes only a few hours – is like arriving at its replica. St. Petersburg and Helsinki, the most beautiful large cities in the North, designed by the same city-planners, built or heavily influenced by the same architects – and during certain periods ruled by the same Tzar, with the same administrative-bureaucratic system and with the same type of prisons.

For my first lecture ever in Finland, I had prepared myself with facts and figures. It was in the sixties. Finland had at that time 160 prisoners per 100,000 inhabitants, compared to between 44 and 69 in Denmark, Sweden and Norway. I can still remember the disbelief expressed by one of the professors of penal law who was present when I presented my figures: Are we in Finland really that far away from the rest of the Nordic countries? It was a shock to him as to several others in the audience.

Why?

For political reasons. Little Finland, close to the USSR, common history, unsafe destiny. In this situation, Finland sought protection, cultural protection, by going west, building links with Scandinavia, becoming Scandinavian. Prisons are cultural symbols. The intellectual-administrative élite with particular responsibility for the crime policy of Finland took action. Year after year Inkeri Anttila, Patrik Tørnudd, and K.J. Lång pressed forward with a penal policy which, in the end, resulted in the prison figure on our map. They accomplished a reduction in the intake to prisons; laws were changed, fines were used more often, prisons less. Prison figures are no artefacts; they are transmitted through important actors, who reflect major values and goals of their times.

And we met these people and their like, continually, in all sorts of Nordic criminological or legal associations. We met for serious scientific tasks, but, at the very same time, we were also building a common culture. It was a strenuous task, particularly for the Finns. We spoke Scandinavian at our meetings, the Danes Danish, the Norwegians Norwegian, the Swedes Swedish. Academics in these three countries understand each other relatively easily. But not the Finns. They struggled through in Swedish, their second language. Swedish was at that time a symbol of belonging to Scandinavia. It was also the important link with the West. A link less provocative to Stalin than if it had been English or German.

Today, this is all about to change. More and more, the Finns present their papers in English. Finland has become a member of NATO and of the European Community. Symbols of belonging to Scandinavia in language as well as in penal policy might not be so important any more. The effects of this on the prison population of Finland remain to be seen – some of the Scandinavians from the 1960s are still in power.

4.5 The Baltic test

Against this background, it is of great interest to watch developments in the Baltic countries. These are countries with considerable similarities to the situation in Finland. Close to Russia, and scared by that closeness, and with strong wishes to create alliances with the Nordic countries across the Baltic Sea, an extensive cultural and economic co-operation takes place. But as we saw from the map, we find an essential difference when we compare the prison populations in Scandinavia with those in the Baltic countries.

So, in my corner of the world, the question is: where will these Baltic countries now move to find a model for the development of their penal system – towards the West, to their Scandinavian neighbours; or towards the North East, their Russian neighbour? My suggestions to Baltic colleagues are influenced by the experiences in Finland. During seminars and meetings with colleagues from the Baltic countries, I try to formulate thoughts about a choice of cultural identity. The penal development in the Baltic countries moves at present in the opposite direction to the one that took place in Finland. Are they aware of the consequences of this? Maybe these countries have to decide. It is very clear that they want to resume their links with the west and the south in general culture, but when it comes to penal policy, is it then still the Russian connection that counts? Or, from a Scandinavian perspective, is it possible to be embraced in very close political-cultural co-operation, but to remain wide apart when it comes to the delivery of pain?

4.6 Tolerance from above

That little country of the Netherlands, densely populated, highly industrialized, with big religious and ethnic divisions, nonetheless – until recently – has had one of the smallest prison populations in Europe. It was a mystery. This low level had been one of the important arguments in the European debate on the necessity of prisons. If the Netherlands could make it, why not also the rest of Europe?

Louk Hulsman (1974) described the level of leniency at that point in time where the number of prisoners was close to its lowest:

> ... the decline in the prison population is attributable not to a drop in the number of custodial sentences imposed but solely to a reduction of their duration. Their relative briefness and the continuing trend to shorten them still further may perhaps be termed the principal characteristic of recent

Dutch penal developments. Only thirty-five sentences of three years or more were passed in 1970, of which fourteen were for homicide (though sixty-three persons were convicted of that crime in that year), two for rape (total number of convictions: sixty-eight), thirteen for robbery with violence, and the remaining six for burglary in combination with extortion ... Parole is almost invariably granted and is not conditional upon the prisoner's willingness to participate in rehabilitation programs (p. 14).

David Downes (1988) described some of the mechanisms which made this possible. The Netherlands had suffered war and occupation. Several of the leading academics experienced life as prisoners. They came out of it with a strong conviction of the negative effects of imprisonment. There were many teachers of penal law among them. These became teachers of the danger of severe prison sentences, and this penetrated the whole penal establishment, not least the police, as many representatives of law and order visiting the Netherlands have experienced.

But in Belgium and France, leading academics were also imprisoned during the Second World War. They, too, had their bad experiences. Yet the prison figures in their countries have not been visibly reduced as a result. Why is there this difference?

David Downes points to the tradition of tolerance in the Netherlands. Louk Hulsman (1974) agrees and uses the weigh-house at Oudewater near Gouda as a symbol for it. At the time of the great witch-hunts in seventeenth-century Europe, people came from near and far to Oudewater to prove that they were not weightless – as witches at that time were supposed to be. In Oudewater, they got a certificate of weight, safeguarding them from prosecution both there and elsewhere. Rutherford (1984, p. 137) quotes a source from 1770 stating that more criminals were executed in London in a year than had been executed in all of Holland for twenty years.

In addition to tolerance, comes a peculiar Dutch mechanism for coping with conflicts. The history of that country is filled with external as well as internal conflicts. The people have learned to live with their internal differences. They have learned the art of compromise. One mechanism to escape conflict has been to delegate decision-making to the top of the system. Here representatives of the opposing forces in

Dutch society are given the mandate to sort out their differences and to come up with solutions that can be lived with by all the various parties. It is an undemocratic solution, but preferable to civil war at a local level. Crime control has been organized according to the same principles. The Dutch have no lay judges. It is a highly professionalized system. Representatives of law and order have been given the mandate to cope with crime according to their own views of what is necessary. That has given them extraordinary powers. With the experience of the Second World War in mind, they have used this power to resist the expansion of the crime control industry.

But they were not alone. Parliament was there. According to Hulsman (1974):

> The debate in the Dutch parliament on the Ministry of Justice budget for 1947 was of unusual interest in that a clear majority urged the government to reconsider its basic position with regard to the penal question. The majority view being that the penal system constitutes a social problem in itself, the government was requested to prepare a concrete plan for tackling this fundamental matter.

But a system based on tolerance from above is a vulnerable one. As David Downes points out (p. 74):

> The major price, so to speak, for such an arrangement is that the élites, both in and outside government and Parliament, are relatively insulated from criticism, except in exceptional circumstances.

And now these exceptional circumstances seem to have gone. Their prison figures have reached the level of their neighbours, and Europe has lost its most spectacular case of tolerance.

What has happened?

Certainly the Netherlands has been under extraordinary international pressure to change its drug policy in a more severe direction; Germany and Sweden in particular have long claimed that the Netherlands is the weak link in the drug defence of Europe. Although David Downes shows that this is not quite true, the pressure may nonetheless have affected penal policy. The situation may have been felt as an embarrassment to the experts within the establishment. As in all other European countries, these experts become increasingly linked to their opposite numbers in the international system, and may slowly come to share their frame of reference. The Dutch representatives become personal objects of international irritation because of their drug policy.

The country is adapting to European standards in other aspects, too. The old divisions have faded away. This probably makes it less important to give a mandate to those at the top to solve all sorts of problems isolated from the population. Crime policy becomes less of a matter for experts – the mass media start to interfere, and demands on the politicians from the general population are more strongly felt. The old divisions dissolve and make room for new: this time the divisions between ordinary people and those seen as criminals.

Another factor is the de-escalation of welfare benefits. Hulsman lists with pride several of these benefits in his 1974 article, and claims that they are behind the exceptional mildness of the Dutch system. Today (oral communication), he explains its increased severity by the absence of several of these benefits.

Also worth mentioning are two developments related to the universities of the Netherlands. A generation of law professors has been replaced; the veterans have left their chairs, taking with them their personal experience and influence. Changes have also taken place in criminology. The Netherlands was the stronghold of criminology in Europe. Most universities had chairs in criminology, or their chairs in penal law were filled with people whose major interests lay in criminology. The criminology of the Netherlands was also of a peculiar kind. It was a critical criminology, more interested in raising questions than in giving answers of immediate use to the authorities. It was also a criminology with exceptionally strong links to humanistic and cultural activities. According to van Swaaningen, Blad and van Loon (1992), several of the criminologists were rather successful novelists or poets. Recently, this whole tradition has sharply declined in the Netherlands. Chairs in criminology have been left empty, and whole institutes have been abolished. Instead, research close to the government has grown rapidly. At the ministerial research and documentation centre, there are at present as many criminologists employed as at all the universities together. It is difficult to know if this development is an effect or a cause of what is happening in the penal area.

4.7 Welfare states at the brink

The situation in the old welfare states is one of unstable equilibrium. Most resistant against destruction are probably those countries with relatively stable economies, long traditions as welfare states, and small and homogeneous populations. Affluence provides scope for tolerance, tradition makes it less offensive to share, and small and homogeneous populations create restraints against excluding people in perceived need. It also helps to stabilise an unstable situation if society recognises several different criteria for goals in life, and has some regard for the "poor but pure", or for generosity rather than efficiency.

But homogeneous small-scale states are also under pressure. They are having to use more money on welfare. *Table 4.7-1* illustrates developments in Norway from 1970 to 1997. Norway is, due to the oil, in an exceptionally good economic situation. Nonetheless, indicators on unemployment, disability pensions and social care show considerable increase in this period. These are the concrete problems. Aggravating them is the fact that the welfare states, too, are troubled by all the organizational principles forced on them by industrialization. Growth takes place in the centres, division of labour becomes a necessity, insurance companies replace mutual aid, and impersonal relations play a greater part. These developments erode much of the moral basis of

Table 4.7-1. Strains on welfare.

	Persons receiving unemployment benefits, per 100,000 population	Persons receiving disability pension per 100,000 population	Cases of social care per 100,000 population
1970	205	3332	1000
1975	379	3548	1200
1980	445	3903	1500
1985	1246	4535	2600
1990	2740	5517	3900
1995	3074	5435	3945
1997	1944	5450	3577

the welfare principles. At the same time, these changes are also among the driving forces behind the steady increase in the amount of crime registered by the authorities. They are also behind the decrease in reports of crimes against honour.

In this new situation, even the most established among welfare states face temptations, temptation to protect themselves, or the social service agencies, rather than those in need.

Several major lines of defence have been drawn up. One is within social welfare itself. Social workers create more and more distance between themselves and those in need of welfare. Workers at municipal social service centres protect themselves against their clients; they keep the centres open for applicants only a few days a week, and on those days only at certain hours every morning, so that people in need line up from 5 a.m. to get access. Telephones are not answered, private police patrol the premises, ordinary police are called in if the social workers feel threatened, as they of course are likely to feel, given the unfamiliarity created by this distance from their clients.

Additional problems are created by the so-called "de-institutionalization" movement. In particular, this is a movement bound to exert pressure on the level of imprisonment in these welfare states in the future. The trend here, like everywhere else, is towards "normalisation". Mental institutions and special schools have been abolished. The slogan is "back to normality". This may have two consequences: Some extraordinary people may be unable to cope, and therefore end up in prison. But another aspect is also important. De-institutionalization does not mean that the institutions disappear. They remain empty, and their former staff remain empty-handed. This creates both a pressure and a temptation. Some of these buildings can easily be converted into prisons, and the staff into prison officers.

4.8 Will it last?

The low punitive level in these archetypes of welfare states is threatened by several forces. Some are of a general character. They have to do with the effects of industrialization, the labour market, and national conflicts. They will be considered in the following chapters. But some are specifically linked to developments in or close to the institution of penal law. These forces will be discussed in what now follows.

My first point is that the joint moral community among those responsible for the penal policy in these countries is under severe strain. 1968 and the student revolt meant a certain democratisation. It meant greater attention given to the rights of certain groups among the weak and the vulnerable. But at the very same time, it also meant increased influence at all levels of the penal establishment. As a part of the general democratisation, these practitioners create their own labour organizations and pressure groups vis-à-vis the political authorities. The prison officers in Norway have blocked the trend towards two in each cell,[4] but are lobbying for more prisons. The police organizations are also working for expansion. A century back they were the mute tools of politicians. Conditions have improved, and deteriorated.

Internationalisation is another strain on the low level of pain-delivery. In the old days, cosmopolitans were also active. Lombroso and Ferri from Italy, and later, von Lizt from Germany were well-known figures in the Nordic debates. As Nauke (1982) and Radzinowicz (1991b) have documented, the stated goals for the International Association of Criminal Policy, and the ideas of von Lizt in particular, contained germs for what developed in Germany after 1933. The effects of these ideas on Scandinavia are unclear. The general decline in prison figures came to an end at the turn of the century. It might have ended without help from abroad. One major result of the various international contacts was the creation of several types of so-called "special measures" of enforced treatment or education, or long-term internment of those supposed to be non-improvable. It has taken most of a century to get rid of the majority of these measures.

---

4 The importance of this fight for the preservation of the principle of one person to one cell is put in perspective by a description of British conditions (Stern 1989, p. 6):
In 1966 Lord Mountbatten said: "It should be more widely known than it is that there are still thousands of prisoners sleeping three in a cell designed in the nineteenth century for one man." More than twenty years later things are no better. In these very same cells, built over a hundred years ago for one person, 5,000 prisoners are living three to a cell and nearly 14,000 are living two to a cell.

Today, internationalisation has moved downwards to the practitioners in the prisons, the probation service, and the police. Increasingly, these practitioners relate to their peers abroad, acquire reference groups in the large and tough countries, obtain information on how the world "really is", and can more easily shrug off criticism from the "theoreticians" whom they see as living their "unreal" lives in ivory towers.

A further strain on the values which keep prison figures low, is created by the penetration of management ideology into state administration. The old personnel saw themselves as civil servants with a major obligation towards a complex set of rules. Often enough, they were caricatured as disappearing behind mountains of documents, slow, but reliable. With management orientation, simplified goals of concrete results and productivity are gaining more weight. What Feeley (1991b) calls "the new penology" with a focus on management of aggregate populations, can also be seen in Scandinavian bureaucracies. But again: This is not a completely dominant theme. A recent trend in Scandinavia, as in Western Europe in general, has been populist demands for law and order. Crime becomes more and more important both in the media and for politicians. In this situation, it is as if the old spirit of the independent class of civil servants has reappeared. British prison governors staged a protest against developments within their service. In Norway, top civil servants within the prison system tell politicians that more prisons and prisoners is not the solution. The police attempt to calm panic, and argue for a balanced approach to problems that exist in all modern states.

The management ideology is also an element within the universities. From the top, the university administration demands planning, efficiency and reports of goals reached. And from the bottom, the students demand useful knowledge, that is knowledge their coming masters – the managers within state and business – will demand from them. This means that the old university standards of critical thinking come under strain. Students become more interested in being equipped with answers that solve administrative problems than with critical questions which only complicate the tasks of those with administrative responsibilities. The moral power of the question-makers is thus diminished.

On the other hand, critical universities and critics within universities have not disappeared completely. In Great Britain, Rutherford (1984) is a leading advocate for what he calls a reductionist agenda. Of central importance in this agenda is the proposal that the physical capacity of the prison system should be substantially reduced – down to 50 percent is his suggestion:

> The reductionist target for the early 1990s should not be around 52,000 as planned by the Home Office, but 22,000 or, in terms of the prison population rate per 100,000 inhabitants, not 110 but in the region of 35.

Lack of belief in prisons in Europe has also been stimulated by Mathiesen's book *Prison on Trial. A Critical Assessment* (1990). The traditional arguments for imprisonment are here analysed and refuted, and we are instead presented with radical alternatives to imprisonment. The books by Rutherford and Mathiesen, and they are not the only ones, exemplify cultural views that are still valid in Western Europe.

The most radical alternative to penal law has been the writings – and even more the teaching – of Louk Hulsman from Rotterdam. His major theme has been an attempt to bring unwanted acts from the domain of penal law over to civil law. In harmony with this approach, he sees penal law not as a solution, but as a social problem in itself. Thus, the goal is not only to limit the use of imprisonment, but also to abolish penal law altogether. Or, in the words of another Dutchman, Willem de Haan (1991):

> Abolitionism (as this tradition of thinking is often called. N.C.) is based on the moral conviction that social life should not and, in fact, cannot be regulated effectively by criminal law and that, therefore, the role of the criminal justice system should be drastically reduced (p. 203).

> ... This is not to deny that there are all sorts of unfortunate events, more or less serious troubles or conflicts which can result in suffering, harm or damage to a greater or lesser degree. These troubles are to be taken seriously, of course, but not as 'crimes' and, in any case, they should not be dealt with by means of criminal law (p. 208).

Personally, I think there are some limits to limits. Without any penal institutions, we might experience a growth in alternatives such as mental hospitals or seemingly benign arrangements which in reality were more oppressive than those we meet in present penal law. My position would be a minimalistic one: that is, as few prisoners as possible, rather than an abolitionistic one. But this discussion is no more than a warning against a deluge in the Sahara. Our major problem is one of limiting increases in the prison populations. Let us turn to that problem.

Chapter 5

Why are there so many prisoners?

5.1 The surplus population

Place: A large industrial town somewhere in Europe.

Time: A day in September, pleasant, sunny, not warm, not cold, ideally suited just to hang around. Which was exactly what so many did most of that day. Not in pubs or coffee-places, but on street corners, close to parking lots, or on some of the empty fields where old houses had been demolished and no new ones had been raised.

Colour: Grey. The sun was out, but was not real. People were grey. The houses were grey, dust and litter and misery reigned in the arena.

Most of those hanging around were unemployed. That was the reason for their presence.

Coming from one of those protected corners of the continent where serious unemployment had not yet hit – this was some time ago – I had to control what I knew was a naive urge: To buy 1000 large brooms and then to organize a festival for cleaning up the place and the atmosphere. One broom to each man, for they were mostly men – the females were of course at home caring for house and children – and then we could have wiped away some of the greyness, the dust, the dirt, the misery.

But of course, I knew this was naiveté, and did not do it. I knew that unemployment has nothing to do with the lack of tasks in urgent need of being done. Unemployment does not mean lack of work, it means lack of *paid* work. Unemployment is an organizational problem – one with severe social consequences. It is a question of the distribution of entrance tickets to what, in these cultures, is seen as a major symbol of full membership. It is a question of power to be able to obtain the ticket, or of solidarity in sharing tickets.

This competition for the status of paid work is softened by several mechanisms. Postponed entrance to the labour market, mostly through compulsory education, makes it legitimate to keep youth in consumer roles. Ideas of life-long learning also keep people out of competition for paid work. Early retirement or the liberal use of the criteria "bad health" are other honourable ways out of the rank of paid workers. These mechanisms can all provide means for consumption without a head-on collision with the norms of consumption as the reward for participation in production.

***

"Empty hands" have been a problem since the earliest stages of industrialization. All those drifting around were seen as creating at least two types of troubles: one by their potential for unrest, the other through the dissonance between this enforced lifestyle of unemployment and the official morality of industriousness. The unemployed might come under suspicion for enjoying their destiny. To both problems, houses for "forced labour" represented a solution. But this solution was only a temporary one; the states were poor, the work houses had to be based on private capital, and profit was greater in other types of investments. In Europe, emigration to the USA relieved much of the pressure. The work-houses were abolished. And lastly, stated in all its brutality, World Wars I and II gave periodic relief.

But the basic problem has not gone. On the contrary, new categories are demanding access to what is seen as a full life. Females are moving back into the market for paid work – just where they were in the beginning of industrialization. Justice for females in societies organized like ours, creates complications for lower class males.[1]

---

1 Cf. Harris (1981) on the situation for black males from the working class in the USA.

In addition, comes what now occurs in Eastern Europe. With all the defects of the old regimes, they had nonetheless a strength in not accepting unemployment. It was, under the old regime, seen as a prime responsibility for the state to guarantee that paid work was available to all able to work. A non-productive idea, probably. We have all heard stories about over-staffed Eastern factories and offices. But all the same, this was an arrangement which prevented unemployment. It meant a guarantee of the right to share one of the most important tools for dignity among humans. Uneconomical, wasteful, open to fraud and corruption – but still a guarantee. Participation in the work-process was for all.

With this old system gone, Eastern Europe gets Western problems. At the very same time, the most extreme forms of Western belief systems based on the advantages of free competition and letting the market decide, increase their hegemonial grip. There seems to be no alternative. Work was shared in the East. That went wrong. Shared work might be dangerous. We are left with a surplus population, those outside production. And we are left with the classical problem: How to control the dangerous classes? How to control all those who are no longer controlled by work-mates, and who might find it unjust to remain outside the important and dignity-creating activity of production? How to control those who, in addition to all this, are forced to experience considerably lower material standards than those in ordinary work?

5.2 Stocks in life

In those days, when the eye of God was supposed to see everything, benefits for good behaviour were also built into the system. Life did not end at death, rewards or punishments might follow. Even life-style might count. Matthew, chapter 5, verse 3, has this to say:

> Blessed are the poor in spirit, for theirs is the kingdom of heaven.

Some translations even state it more strongly:

> Blessed are the poor, for theirs is the kingdom of heaven.

Theologians disagree on the choice between these two translations. The first one is at present the authorized one. But the second is by far the more powerful when it comes to social control. Here, all the poor get their reward, eventually. Such a society does not necessarily get in trouble with its surplus population. That population can be kept waiting, poor but honest.

But that society is not our society. Ours is founded on a considerable amount of talk about equality in this life, and of dissatisfaction when it becomes clear that this talk is just talk. So, we have to resort to other forms of control.

A basic tenet of social control is that those who own very much and those who own nothing are the two extremes that are the most difficult to govern. Those who own much have power also and are able to resist control; those with little have nothing to lose and little to fear. Jock Young (1989, p. 154) has an important critique of earlier epochs' understanding of poverty:

> The failure of the social democratic consensus of the 1950s that better conditions would reduce crime was based on notions of the reduction of absolute deprivation. But it is not absolute but relative deprivation which causes crime (Lea and Young, 1984). It is not the absolute level of wealth, but resources perceived as unfairly distributed which affect the crime rate.

And Young continues with a prescription for crime prevention which sounds like a list of steps *not* taken in modern welfare states these last years:

> To reduce crime we must reduce relative deprivation by ensuring that meaningful work is provided at fair wages, by providing decent housing which people are proud to live in, by ensuring that leisure facilities are available on a universal basis, and by insisting that policing is equally within the rule of law, both for the working class and middle class, for blacks and for whites.

Balvig (1990, p. 25) points to the basic problem as one of non-usefulness. The message in this development is that there is no longer any reason to believe that the welfare state will provide work for all. Society is gradually changing from having a shared or common rationality into one of individual rationality.

5.3 Drug control as class control

For the police, as for most people, this situation offers no easy answers. The number of reports to the police is increasing rapidly in all industrialized nations. Some call these crimes, some call them complaints. Either way, behind them are acts which range from creating nuisance to causing severe dangers and suffering among people who see no other solution than to address their complaints to the police. But in reality the police can do very little. The quantity of commodities that can be stolen is steadily increasing. There is so much to remove, so much to drink. There are so few people around in the living quarters in the day-time, and too many in the entertainment quarters at night. People do not know each other. The police have no magic available. With the exception of serious cases of violence where all resources are mobilised, they can in such a society solve little more than what is solved by itself. This creates a crisis in state hegemony, says Phillipe Robert (1989, p. 109–110):

> In fact, since the victim usually cannot identify the offender, what else can he or she do but file a complaint? Recourse to the criminal justice system is no longer an element in a strategy; it has become an automatic process for which there is no alternative. ... police action is increasingly half-hearted, since there is no known suspect in most complaints and, as everyone knows, this means that there is hardly any chance of the police solving the case.

In this situation, the war on drugs creates alternative possibilities for control of the dangerous population. The war on drugs is at the same time a war on attributes *correlated* with drug use: being young, being from inner cities, exhibiting life-styles unacceptable to the middle class. By fighting drugs – certain drugs, not alcohol or sleeping pills – a large proportion of the dangerous classes will be in the catch.

But let me add. Behind this view is no theory of conspiracy. There are several rational arguments behind the wish for some sort of control on both the import and the use of drugs, even though the means applied might be debated. That the war against drugs also provides an opportunity to control the dangerous classes in general does not discredit either the original motives or the central persons in the drug war. Consequences are different from reasons.

Especially at the beginning of the war against drugs in Scandinavia, we still believed that we had found the road to the perfect society. We had full employment, free education, free medical services, and a general belief in steady progress. Those who so wished, could work their way into the good, deserved life. But then came drugs. The hippies arrived, and rejected some of the fruits of affluence. After the hippies came the drop-outs among the more addicted. Two interpretations were possible. Maybe there were still defects in the welfare system. Maybe industrialization – even in welfare-states – meant losses to some people. And maybe old social injustices had remained, and the drop-outs represented the old losers in a new form. The alternative interpretation was that the danger lay in the drugs. Drugs were actually so dangerous that they destroyed people even in the most perfect of welfare societies.

It is easy to see which answer was most suitable for those responsible for building the welfare state. A war against drugs was declared. And such a war was not in opposition to welfare, but in harmony with it. One element of welfare is caring for people, caring for them even against their own wishes, and also protecting the vulnerable against the dangers in life.

Later developments have only increased the reasons for a war against drugs. The gaps between classes, even in welfare states run by social democrats, are clearly widening. The number of extremely rich people is increasing, while the living standard of the population in general is under severe strain. This creates a need to keep a distance from the bottom. The strain on the welfare system is also reflected in an increased quota of people on skid row. Poverty has again become visible. Beggars have appeared. The homeless and drug-users are out in the streets. They hang around everywhere, dirty, abusive – provocative in their non-usefulness.

We get a repetition of what happened in the thirties, only more so since the inner cities have been rebuilt since then. Hiding places in slums and dark corners have been replaced by heated arcades leading into glittering shopping paradises. Of course, homeless and/or unemployed persons also seek these public alternatives to the places of work and homes they are barred from. And as an equal matter of course, they are met with agitated demands to get them out of sight and out of mind. Back in the thirties, this was accomplished by seeing similar categories as "sick" and in need of treatment. A special prison was built, where people arrested for drunkenness in the streets were warehoused for long periods under the pretext of treatment for alcohol problems. Similar arrangements existed both in Finland and Sweden. In the 1960s and the 1970s these were all abolished.

Today, newcomers among the unwanted are again seen as sick or at least without ordinary will-power due to their supposedly irresistible demand for drugs. And now these categories are even more suited for penal action. In the thirties, their sickness was seen as related to alcohol, after all a legal substance and used by the majority. Only abuse could be punished, not use. Today, several of their intoxicating substances are illegal (even though the major drug is still alcohol). The illegality creates a clear cut difference between "them" and "us".

In Scandinavia, the war against drugs has to a large extent become a repetition of what Gusfield (1963) describes from the Prohibition Period. The crusade at that time was directed not only against alcohol, but also against new pretenders to the moral hegemony in the USA. In all industrialized societies, the war against drugs has developed into a war which concretely strengthens control by the state over the potentially dangerous classes. They are not challengers, as described by Gusfield, but offensive in lifestyle. Not only are shortcomings in society explained (away), but also, quite concretely, a large segment of the non-productive population is securely placed behind bars. Much of the severe strain on European prisons stems from the war against drugs. So also does the increase in the USA.

The effects on Norway of these developments over the last nineteen years are reflected in *Table 5.3-1*. What I have done here is simply (less simply in practice, though) to count how many years of imprisonment the judges have handed down for each year from 1979 to 1997. As we see, they have nearly doubled the volume of intended years of pain in these nineteen years, from 1,620 to 3,118. The next column contains the drug sentences. Here we find an increase from 219 to 1001 years; that means more than a fourfold increase in these years. And in the last column, we can see how drugs play an increasingly

Table 5.3-1. Number of years of imprisonment decided by the courts each year in Norway from 1979 to 1997. Total number, and for drugs.

Year	Total	Drugs	Percent drugs of total
1979	1620	219	14
1980	1630	245	15
1981	1792	326	18
1982	2073	388	19
1983	2619	650	25
1984	2843	684	24
1985	2522	592	24
1986	2337	458	20
1987	2586	683	26
1988	2688	756	29
1989	3022	832	28
1990	3199	789	25
1991	3319	910	27
1992	3209	869	27
1993	3350	977	29
1994	3517	1083	31
1995	3222	947	29
1996	2873	817	28
1997	3118	1001	32

important part in the pain budget. A third of all the years of intended pain are now for drugs. This development is reflected in our earlier presented *Diagram 4.3–1* on prison growth in Norway in this period. The figures for growth are trifling compared to what we find outside Scandinavia, but we can nevertheless observe a considerable increase – up one-third – in the number of prisoners.

Developments in the USA will be given special attention in Chapters 7 and 8, but already here some elementary figures will be given to illustrate the importance of the war against drugs for prison development. *Diagram 5.3-2* shows the sentenced population of the Federal prisons from 1970 to 1997.

Diagram 5.3-2. Percent of total Federal prison population sentenced for drug offences. USA, 1970–1997.[1]

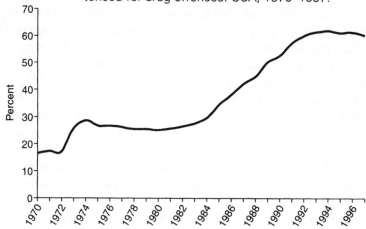

1 Bureau of Justice Statistics 1997, *Table 6.52*, p. 506.

Table 5.3-2 from Mauer (1999) shows State Prison Inmates by Offence 1985–1995. Again we see the effects of the war on drugs.

Table 5.3-2. Increase in new sentences to State prisons by crime type, 1985–95

Offense	Prison Sentences 1985	Prison Sentences 1995	Increase 1985–95	% Increase	% of Total
Total	183,131	337,492	154,361	84%	100%
Violent	64,300	99,400	35,100	55%	23%
Property	77,600	97,600	20,000	26%	13%
Drug	24,200	104,400	80,200	331%	52%
Public order, other	17,100	36,100	19,000	111%	12%

Note: Due to rounding, columns do not add up to 100 %. Data calculated from Bureau of Justice Statistics reports.

***

The war against drugs has in practice paved the way for a war against persons perceived as the least useful and potentially the most dangerous part of the population, those whom Spitzer (1974) calls "social junk", but who actually are seen as more dangerous than junk. They illustrate that everything is not quite as it should be in the social fabric, and at the same time they are a potential source of unrest. In Spitzer's terminology, they become junk and dynamite at the very same time. Through the war against drugs, a pincers movement encircles them. For some of their acts, they are seen as serious criminals. They are called "drug-sharks" and are incarcerated for exceptionally long periods if they import or sell more than minimal amounts of drugs. In reality, most of those thus punished are themselves users, situated at a considerable distance from the top of society (Bødal, 1982). The large-scale dealers from the middle- and upper-classes do exist, even in the prisons, but as rare exceptions. As the other side of the pincers movement, we see initiatives to establish coercive cures. In this connection, mainly the same people are now seen more as miserable misfits. Between the two sides of the pincers movement, they are caught in a firm grip.

5.4 Fortress Europe, Western Division[3]

The first edition of this book was written during one of the most turbulent periods in the history of modern Europe. As I wrote, the USSR came to an end. So also did the iron curtain. At the northern tip of my country, we have a common border with what is now Russia. Without any iron curtain, we have to face the new realities of that neighbourhood.

We do not like everything we see.

It is particularly uncomfortable to get such a clear picture of poverty. Those living close to the border, react as good neighbours. They invite hungry people in, or collect food to send them. But at the state level, it looks different. Russia is so big; what if all those people, or even a fraction of them, got the idea of going west? Those hungry neighbours would certainly eat us out of the house. 2.5 million adults have already decided to go west according to an EEC-study of January 1992. An additional 10.5 million say they will probably decide to go.[4]

3 I am much grateful to Thomas Mathiesen for his help in describing this system. See also his recent book (Mathiesen 2000) on Schengen.
4 *Aftenposten*, January 1992, p. 3.

The problem is similar in countries further down the map. It is the same all around Western Europe. We are surrounded by hungry neighbours. And the solution is clear: that old fence created by Stalin and his likes must be raised once more, this time from the other side of the border, and now also extended to the south. Africa is also hungry. And so is Asia. Fortress Europe is taking shape, Fortress Europe, Western Division.

The ground had already been prepared before the USSR dissolved. Several steps had been taken. The first was symbolised by the letters **TREVI**. This was an intergovernmental forum for the Interior and Foreign Ministers of the European Community. The group had also been given the status of observers in certain other countries, like the United States, Canada, Morocco and the Nordic countries. TREVI stood for **T**errorism, **R**adicalism, **E**xtremism and **V**iolence. The group was set up in 1976, principally to combat terrorism, but the original mandate was later extended to special groups on "Police Co-operation", "Serious Crime and Drug Trafficking", and, last but not least, "Policy and Security Implications of the Single European Market".

The TREVI arrangement is now history in the sense that it has been supplanted by operative organisations. The legal framework for these operations is to a large extent established in the Schengen Agreement. Schengen is a town in Luxembourg, where that country, together with France, West Germany, Belgium and the Netherlands signed in 1985 a formal agreement to abolish their internal border controls ahead of the rest of the European Community. It was seen as a pilot project for the new community. After much disagreement, as well as criticism of the extreme amount of secrecy surrounding the agreement, a detailed Convention was signed in June 1990. The Convention entered into force in seven countries in March 1995. During the following years, all EU countries except Great Britain and Ireland joined in (but they are now on their way), and the non-EU countries Norway and Iceland entered into separate collaborative agreements. At the EU summit in Amsterdam in 1997, Schengen, which all along had been a EU project, was formally integrated into the EU structure, and entered into force on 1 May 1999. In the words of Abel et al. (1991, p. 4):

> ... while yet to be ratified, its provisions on police co-operation and infor-
> mation exchange are the most detailed insight we have on the shape of
> things to come.

And things to come are all in defence of Fortress Europe.

First, the police will be able to cross borders between countries. They will be entitled to carry their own firearms, but entry into private homes and places not accessible to the public is prohibited.

Second, a joint information system will be established (Convention, Art. 92):

> The Schengen Information System shall enable the authorities designated by the Contracting Parties, by means of an automated search procedure, to have access to reports on persons and objects for the purposes of border checks and controls and other police and customs checks carried out within the country ...

New technical tools will also soon be available for this control. In a new criminal justice newsletter, *Europe* (vol. 1, number 1, p. 3) we are told:

> Researchers at Essex University in England are experimenting with a fingerprint scanning system that can be coupled with a credit card to reduce fraud. A model of the device is being tested by a company owned by the University, Essex Electronic Consultants, to resolve problems associated with the device.
> ...
> A scanner at the business location would be used to compare the credit card bearer's fingerprint image with the one imbedded in the card's magnetic strip. In addition to its use to prevent credit card fraud, the technique is believed to have many more applications, including cash machines, drivers' licenses, passports and personal identification.

And third, a tight system of control of foreigners has been established. The external borders can only be crossed at authorized crossing-points. The states will carry out a common policy with regard to people outside Fortress Europe. They will harmonise policies on visa and asylum requests, and exchange information on those seen as not wanted. Entrance can be denied if other "Schengencountries" have negative information on a person. "A no from one country, is a no from twelve. A yes from one, is a yes only from one" (Morén 1991, p. 43). A company carrying a person across a border can be fined if that person is without valid documents.

What does this all add up to ?

A sort of siege. Internal borders are being weakened, but this is compensated for by strengthened internal control in the form of armed police with the authority to cross national borders, and a shared information system; and, as the essential element, a much more efficient system of control at the external borders. The iron curtain is down, up comes the visa curtain.

Maybe Western Europe, at least for some time to come, will be able to preserve a relatively low level of prisoners by keeping what will be seen as the most dangerous elements outside this assembly of affluent societies. Maybe Western Europe for a while can be preserved as an island of welfare by locking the poor out, rather than locking them into the prisons of the Fortress. By waging a war against foreigners, we might also become less preoccupied with the fight against those traditionally perceived as internal enemies. The question is only if the price for this much wanted prison-situation may be too high. Let these last reflections protect us against West European self-satisfaction when we later look into what happens in Russia and on the other side of the Atlantic.

Chapter 6

The Russian case

6.1 The homecomer

When the great Russian singer – and poet, and human being – Vladimir Vysotskij once visited a town containing one of the large car factories in his country, he had to walk down the long street from the railway station to his night quarters (Palmær 1986, p. 10). As he moved along, one window after another was opened, tape recorders were placed in them, and his songs beamed out in full volume throughout the route. It was like the home-coming of an emperor.

Vysotskij gave words to the experience of millions of Russians. He grew up close to one of the central railway stations in Moscow, *Rizjskij Vokzal*. The area was overcrowded in the extreme. Up to 20 families might share one apartment and one toilet. This was the time of the big amnesties after Stalin's death. The prisoners came home. They told their tales, sang their sorrows. Vysotskij listened, and brought their words to the world.

In the 1950s, some 2.5 million prisoners were in the GULAGS of the USSR. We tend to think of them as political prisoners. GULAGS were the camps for a Solszhenitsyn, for a Irina Ratusjinskaja (1988) with "Grey is the colour of hope", and for all of their like. And indeed, they formed a large contingent, the political prisoners, the "class enemies", those with the wrong opinions, the wrong families, and the wrong class or connections. But then, as now, the camps would also have been for the more ordinary sorts of people, who under more ordinary conditions are put in ordinary prisons, mental hospitals or youth institutions. These were the people who – if they were permitted to return home after the amnesties – went home to Moscow or St. Petersburg, and moved in among those others at the bottom of the social system.

They must have been the same sort of people as those who now come home from the prisons and camps in the USA. Home to the inner cities of Washington, Baltimore, Los Angeles. Among the poor, few families in Moscow would be without members with experience of life in the camps. Among the poor in the inner cities of USA, the situation must be the same. In both nations, this is the breeding ground for another culture. For Vysotskij and his less famous equals in Russia. For ICE-T and his equals in the USA.

Vysotskij's songs have the melancholy of Russia. Their equivalents from the USA sound to my ears more pulsating, faster, more aggressive. I am not sufficiently tuned into the US rap-scene to analyze similarities and dissimilarities in the music from Moscow/St.Petersburg versus Los Angeles/New York. A superficial impression is that Vysotskij's songs are more sad, without hope, but sometimes with strong themes of rebellion, as in his famous "The Wolf-hunt". These political messages seem less clear in the US equivalents. But some of the themes are much the same: despair, distance from loved ones, friendship, ecstasy, with tragedy as the inevitable outcome.

6.2 Prisons for labour

All the way up to the last stages of the old regimes in Eastern Europe, several of their prison systems were run at a profit. Work morale was low both inside and outside of prison, but much easier to control inside. I remember a visit to a model prison in Poland before democratisation. From the top floor there were factories as far as the eye could see. These factories were all inside a massive wall, and belonged to the prison. According to the vice-director of the prison administration for the whole country, the system as a whole was run with a considerable profit. Even around 1990, this was the case. The Helsinki Watch (1991, p. 36) had this to say after a long and detailed study of Prison Conditions in the Soviet Union:

Prisoners receive a wage from which is deducted money to pay for their upkeep. They can perform services for the colony, such as cleaning, cooking, maintenance or providing medical care (if they are properly qualified) or else they can work in the production facility of the camp. Carpentry, furniture-making, metalworking, and simple electronics are some of the industries found in the colonies. Prison production is sold to the general public and was until recently exported to "fraternal socialist countries". It is unclear how the export of prison products has been affected by the downfall of most of the communist governments in Eastern Europe and by a reorientation of Soviet trading relations toward hard currency transactions, but one press report noted an effort by prisons to enter into joint ventures with Western European firms. Prison production is a vital part of the Soviet economy, accounting for 8.5 billion rubles of revenue per year. In 1989, profits from prison production amounted to 1.14 billion. In some areas, prisons are monopoly producers, particularly in agricultural machinery.

The colonies had a central role in the Russian economy. They were among the best functioning parts of the old economy. Here was a captive work force, sober, well-ordered, working in two shifts in factories inside the same fence. As stated with pride in a colony I visited: "Had it not been for the heavy taxes we pay to the state, this colony, even with the pay given to both guards and prisoners, would have gone with a profit last year." And outside the windows of the director's office were stored the reasons for his pride: the farm machinery produced in this colony.

These products were the pride of the colony, but also a potential danger for the whole system. Recently, they had not been able to find customers for their products. They produced for storage. Nor had they been able to find anybody who would receive their prisoners on release. Again a quotation: "In the old days, we could just tell a factory that they had to hire a prisoner who was to be released next month. Today, we have nobody to tell."

6.3 Stored away

Ironically, the situation for those waiting for trial is worst for Russian prisoners. These prisoners are mostly placed in rather old-fashioned prisons in urban areas. The conditions in these overcrowded prisons are extremely unsatisfactory, cf. King (1994). After being sentenced, nearly all prisoners are transferred to corrective labour colonies, the former GULAGS. These colonies are dormitories or barracks built together with factories. According to Western standards, conditions in the colonies are also cramped, but considerably less so than in the pre-trial prisons. Helsinki Watch (1991) had this to say about living conditions in the prisons ten years back (pp. 14–15):

> Conditions in the pre-trial detention centres are appalling. Those we saw were all overcrowded, airless, hot in summer, cold in winter and usually smelly. Butyrskaia in Moscow, originally built hundreds of years ago as a fortress, has a capacity of 3,500.[1] On June 11, 1991, when we visited, it had 4,100 inmates, of which some 250–300 were convicted criminals with pending appeals. Krasnopresneskaia, with a capacity of 2,000, always has 2,200–2,300; when we visited, it had 2,264. "Two hundred and sixty-four have no place to sleep," the prison chief told us, "and must sleep either sideways or on the floor." The notorious Kresty detention centre, the larger of two serving the 5 million people in the Petersburg area, has a capacity of 3,300 but a population of 6,000–6,500! "The further one gets from Moscow," one official told us, "the worse things get."

A team from the Danish newspaper Politiken[2] confirms the report from the Kresty prison in St. Petersburg. Kresty means cross, and this seems appropriate as a metaphor for a prison with up to 14 inmates in cells of eight square meters.

> "My whole body hurts because I can never stretch my legs or back," said a tall, young lad. He was the last arrival, and had therefore to sleep close to the door and the open toilet.

Or again in the words from Helsinki Watch (p. 15):

> Inmates sit or lie on their beds, often bent over if on the bottom bunk. The windows are shut, or if they are open, they are so blocked by metal bars or blinds that no light or air gets in. The doors are solid, with only a peephole or sometimes a slot through which food can be passed. Ventilation is virtually non-existent; the cells are hot in the summer and cold in the winter, and are often only dimly lit.

---

1 Since 10–15 percent of a prison's cells are usually under repair or used for other than regular housing, the actual capacity is closer to 3,000.
2 *Politiken,* Copenhagen, 10 May, 1992.

Prison authorities are desperate, but with few possibilities for reform. "I know how a prison ought to be," said the director to the journalists. "I have been on a study-tour to Finland. But to us, such conditions are just a dream."

I expressed considerable pessimism in the first edition of this book. And today, preparing the third edition, I can only say that the situation has deteriorated further. Conditions in the colonies are bad, conditions in some of the pre-trial prisons are of a sort that is virtually beyond description. In Moscow, I met 57 persons in a room the size of a small class-room, confined there day and night, sleeping in three shifts, packed together in the beds, with wide-spread sickness, a scarcity of food, dependence on gifts from relatives outside, and an extreme scarcity of fresh air. "One year here is as three in the colonies," said several prisoners.

What is worse, conditions are deteriorating. After the economic crisis during the summer of 1998, the Russian State is out of money. The state allots two-thirds of a ruble per day per prisoner. This amount is also for medicine. Twenty rubles in the summer of 1998 were equal to one dollar.

6.4 TB

What is also new, at least in its dimensions, is tuberculosis.

Among the one million prisoners in 1999, 92,000 are estimated to have this sickness. Some have received some treatment, but it is inadequate. Ordinary TB has developed into multi-resistant TB among 30,000 of the prisoners. A prison sentence means a sentence with a heavily increased risk of TB and death, or in the words of Farmer (1998), this is a situation with "Drug-Resistant Tuberculosis as Punishment".

Vivien Stern (1999) reports that there are 45 special TB colonies. One is in Marininsk in Siberia, 5000 km from Moscow. The chief doctor from the colony approached Doctors without Borders and asked for help. A young Belgian doctor, Hans Kluge, took up the invitation and arrived in Marininsk in 1996. Speaking at a seminar in 1998 organised by the International Centre for Prison Studies, he described the obstacles he faced (Stern pp. 3–4):

> Patients arrive in Marininsk in a very advanced state. It is very overcrowded – and there is no isolation. Patients put their sputum everywhere. ... Our problems are increased by the existence of the internal hierarchy (a caste-system operating among the prisoners. N.C.) ... We forced them to drink the milk whilst we were watching because the lowest people in the hierarchy were beaten up and lost their milk. When we first arrived in the prison, we treated some of the prisoners for scabies, but we found that there was considerable opposition to this from the prisoners themselves. We later discovered that having scabies was considered to be good protection against being gang-raped in the showers.
> ...
> We have a cure rate of 40 percent which is unacceptable. ... These are juveniles (14–18) ... All those still infected after four months are put in one department because they might have multi-drug resistant TB. We then put a fence between all the departments. We put the chronics behind a fence with barbed wires and soldiers – this is a terrible thing to have to do on the verge of the 21st century – I have to go in and look these people in the eyes.

Dr. Kluge became TB positive whilst working in the colony.

Vivien Stern underlines that the problem is not just in the prisons. Prisoners leave and return to their homes and their communities. There is no system of follow-up. Speaking at a press conference, Nathalya Vezhnina from Marininsk said:

> Each year 600 people are released from our colony. They carry the problem with them into society. These are people who have active tuberculosis, who can themselves infect up to 100 people a year.

In the Swedish newspaper *Dagens Nyheter* (9 August, 1999) Kluge shows the consequences of this:

> Each year 300,000 Russian prisoners are released. About 10,000 have multi-resistant tuberculosis. If we calculate that each of them has the possibility to contaminate 20 persons, Russia will have two million cases of this type of tuberculosis within ten years.

Imprisonment before being sentenced is particularly dangerous. The

Moscow Centre for Prison Reform (Abramkin 1998) gives this description of the conditions in the prisons for those awaiting trial – the SIZO-prisoners:

> In the SIZOs of larger populated areas each prisoner is allocated less than 1 sq.m. of space, in some cells it is less than 0.5 sq.m. Prisoners have to sleep in turns. There is no room for all inmates to sit there. Conditions in SIZO cells are extremely harsh: lack of oxygen, dampness, stench. Many inmates have bloody ulcers and legs swollen from long periods of standing, many are infected with scabies and other skin diseases. Their bodies are perspiring and nothing can dry due to the humidity. There is practically no light that enters through the heavily barred window. Two or three-tier beds are fastened to the walls. Any cell, be it for 10 or 100 inmates, has one sink and one toilet (p. 31).

I would not have believed it, if I had not been there myself, seen it, smelled it. The description needs only to be combined with our knowledge of tuberculosis: In a closed and non-ventilated room for more than 100 prisoners, inevitably some will be among the infected and cough out their sputum.

Compared to these conditions, it sounds as the utmost hypocrisy when Western Europe is preoccupied with the task of forcing Russia to abolish the use of the death-penalty. If Russia and its neighbours do not stop executing their prisoners, the state will not get access to the European Council. Russia has succumbed to that pressure. No one is executed in Russia these days. They just die.

6.5 Counter-forces

The former prisoners of the GULAGS had one stroke of good luck: They had prisoners among them easily seen as political. Not by the regime – by the power holders they were seen as more criminal than any, just by having committed crimes against the regime. But slowly, more and more perceived it otherwise. Little by little, the GULAGS gained the meaning of being work-camps for unwanted persons. In the end, they became symbols of political oppression. When the political regime became slightly less harsh after Stalin, and likewise the internal regime in the GULAGS, all those living there shared some of the benefits. Those seen as the "pure" politicians, functioned as the engine for reforms for the benefit of the many. Political reforms acquired criminal-political consequences.

But today? The political element is solidly buried. Crime has got the upper hand, in the meaning given to deviant acts committed by those males who are without paid work. In Russia as in the USA. The political establishment in Russia has re-directed its attention to what always has been in the centre of Russian politics: the struggle between the factions at the top of society. Little political attention is given those at the bottom of society, nor are there resources for social reforms. Seeing their acts as crimes, followed by transport to the colonies, is the major remaining alternative.

But this is too grim a picture. There are also counter-forces at play. There are civil servants of high quality working in the Russian system. They see the overcrowding as a major problem, and work, dedicated to reducing the number of prisoners. There are reports from the colonies of directors who, against all odds, are turning the places into selfsufficient units, and from other colonies of staff sharing the living conditions with the inmates. And lastly, in the new political situation in Russia, new pressure-groups are appearing. One of the most important is probably the Moscow centre for prison reform,[3] which runs its own radio station, publishes pamphlets and books, arranges national and international meetings. One of its last accomplishments was a large photo exhibition: The entrance hall of the Russian Duma (Parliament) was last winter (1998/1999) filled with pictures of the conditions inside Russian prisons and the colonies. The delegates had to pass the body-sized pictures of misery every day they came to their place of work. Pictures do not smell, but the inmates on these pictures came very close.

Maybe this pressure is behind a surprise visit Prime Minister Vladimir Putin paid to the Kresty prison September 1999. According to *Mir za Nedelyu* (The world this week) Sept. 16–23: "Although always demure, Putin was shocked by the prison interior of Kresty. There is not such a lack of space even in the prisons of China, was his conclusion."

3 Their leader is Valery Abramkin, a dissident who spent six years in prisons and colonies, and who has not forgotten.

6.6 Dangers ahead

Nonetheless, the outcome is not clear. The dangers ahead in Russia relate to six basic features:

First: Russia has built up a large prison industry which earlier was of great importance for the economy. With the market economy and privatisation, this prison industry is not able to compete. The tradition of maintaining a large prison population is well-established, but the profit from this arrangement has gone. One possible consequence of this is a further detoriation of living conditions within the prisons.

Second: the country has an administrative structure and a tradition very much adapted to the enormous prison figures. At the administrative level, Russia has still a "commando administration". It is an enormously centralised one, based on control from the top and on detailed regulations on what those lower down have to do. Functionaries in the system – and police and prosecutors are among them – have to fill specified quotas for performance, the number of arrests, the number of sentences. And this relates to advancement. There are no great incentives to keep people out of prison if the measure of success – and criteria for advancement – is the number you are able to get into prison. This is combined with a cultural tradition where the prosecutors are very powerful in comparision with the judges. It is not common for a judge to go directly against a prosecutor and free a suspect. A better solution, for the officials involved, is for the case to be sent back to the prosecutor for further investigation – while the suspect is sent back to the same old prison for further waiting. Nor is it good for the lower judge to come out with lenient decisions which on appeal are changed to harsher ones. It is better for the junior to show strength by tough decisions, and eventually risk the senior judges showing signs of leniency.

All this is particularly reflected at the pre-trial stage. The average length of pre-trial detention is ten months, and a considerable percentage of prisoners await a court decision from one to six years according to Abramkin (1998, p. 64). Formally, prisoners cannot be kept without trial for more than one and a half years, but there are no limits on how long a trial can last, and the prisoners can remain in SIZO for that whole period. Abramkin adds:

Yet, the main reason for overcrowding in SIZOs remains the law-and-order stance of the Russian authorities. Numerous, arbitrary arrests and crackdowns overwhelm a system with no money for maintaining present prisoner population levels, let alone for paying staff and constructing new prisons. Yet the present crime-fighting policy is unfocused in its provision of basic security for the population. ... the state still refuses to make a distinction between more and less harmful categories of crime.

Third: all this happens in a system which is understaffed and without material resources. Thereby vicious circles are created. There is a lack of legal staff to handle the large numbers, and there is a lack of room for them when they want to meet their clients in the prison.

Fourth: the external situation is one where the pressure to contain the unwanted parts of the population is at a maximum. Russia has adopted elements of economic thinking from the West, and a media industry that makes money from writing on crime. But there is no safety-net for protecting those falling outside the system, and there is no efficient control of the new entrepreneurs.

Fifth: there exists a deep ambivalence in Russia in respect to the market economy and the resulting changes. Life is difficult, conditions have not changed with the promised speed, and much of the discomfort needs an explanation. "The Mafia" is a handy one. Bäckman (1998 a and b), suggests that the image of the Russian Mafia has probably given more income to Hollywood than to those who are supposed to be running the system in Russia. Rawlinson (1998) describes (pp. 354–355) how the media struggle to present a dramatised picture of "Mafia-types":

> The demand for interviews with Russian gangsters far outweighs the supply and has consequently spawned a new industry for the ever-watchful entrepreneur. Low-ranking gang members, and even 'straight' guys play 'hood' for journalists in return for high interview fees.

In other words, the Mafia image is a useful one. Useful for the film-industry, useful for the media, useful for ordinary, deprived people who want to understand why those who were seen as criminals in the old days suddenly are at the top of the pleasant life, and useful as an explanation of the misery. In addition, the Mafia image is also a highly useful tool for the Russian authorities for giving power back to the Ministry of the Interior, and in particular to the various branches of the police.

There exists, of course, organised crime in Russia, both at the social top and bottom levels. But the problem is much more complex than is usually stated. We do not here need to go deeper into it. Here, it suffices to conclude that *belief* in the Mafia is a social fact with considerable consequences – for the prison population as well. Big shots are rarely imprisoned. But they legitimize a war against them, a war where a large number of small people are kept in prison for extremely long periods.[4]

Sixth, and final point: A growth-inducing factor in the Russian prison population is the many reformers from the West, with their message for the Russians that they also have to fight crime, and particularly drugs, as we do. Look to Scandinavia, or to the USA! Quite recently I visited a powerful member of the Duma. He must have been, as he had so many telephones on his desk in one of the two enormous offices he had at his disposal. He gave a long speech on the importance of creating a drug-free Russia. One addict recruits ten new ones, he told us. His ideas had already become the law of the land. The pressure on the prisons by such laws will obviously increase.

***

The serious danger in this whole situation is that the SIZOs will be forced to receive even more prisoners awaiting trial, and that the colonies will lose their production capability and become camps for internment only. Even while recognising the existence of a great degree of idealism and of good intentions within the administration and staff in the Russian prison system, it is to be feared that the life situation for prisoners in Russia will deteriorate to an extent that will influence the whole of Russian society. In addition comes the most recent political development: Vladimir Putin was on March 26 this year (2000) elected as President of Russia. Law and order and the need

4 A more thorough analysis of the Mafia problem is given in an article I have called "A much needed Mafia – on the social function of sloppy terms" (Christie 2000).

for a strong state were his major messages prior to the election. "The stronger the state, the more free are the citizens", was one of his statements. Another one was "Democracy is the dictatorship of the law". Not the most suitable program for keeping the number of prisoners under control.

Chapter 7

USA – the Trend-setter

7.1 Whom one loveth, one chasteneth

There are few countries so pleasant to visit as the USA. As a Norwegian, I feel close to home, sometimes better than at home. We often say that there are as many Norwegians in the USA as there are in Norway. They made a good deal by leaving the old country, materially, and maybe also socially. The warm atmosphere in many encounters, the care for new neighbours, the fascination of the variations within the large cities.

These words are being written in an attempt to counteract any completely wrong interpretations of what now follows. I am intending to do the impossible. I am trying to say that I am fundamentally fond of a country and its people, that I feel close to it, and its national heritage. But at the same time, I will claim that there is something extraordinarily alarming in the social fabric of the USA. And precisely because I feel so close, feel the country as so much of myself, it is increasingly difficult to keep quiet and not express my concern.

Most difficult of all is to meet colleagues from the USA. American criminology rules much of the world, their theories on crime and crime control exert an enormous influence. American criminologists are kind and conscientious people, kind to visitors, conscientious in their standards of scientific activity. Their standards become our standards and their solutions tend to be copied abroad.

Maybe these are the reasons why I think of Germany from the 1920s and later. Germany, that country of culture and insight, that country of science, that country of rational thoughts and romantic hearts. Norway has always been more oriented towards England and the USA than towards Continental Europe. Oceans were better for transport than mountain roads. But respect for Germany was high. Their legal writers were held in high esteem, as well as their general policy on law and order. Scholars went there. Police and prosecution authorities went there. They were the influential model, maybe for a little too long.

Today we go to America.

7.2 The great confinement

In June 1983, *Correctional Magazine* had this to say about the growth in the prison population of the USA:

> "Fantastic ... enormous ... terrifying," were the words chosen by Norval Morris of the University of Chicago Law School to describe last year's increase in the US prison population.
>
> "It's an astonishing increase,"says Alfred Blumstein of Carnegie-Mellon University in Pittsburgh. "We don't have the resources to confine these people, and the cost is going up. There's got to be an explosion."
>
> "I am genuinely surprised; that's stunning growth," says Franklin Zimring, Director of the Center for Studies in Criminal Justice at the University of Chicago.
>
> "It's even worse than what I had expected," says Kenneth Carlson of Abt Associates in Cambridge, Mass. "It becomes more and more frightening."

This is what these experts said about the growth in the prison population up until 1983. At that time the population in Federal and State prisons had reached 419,820; the jails held 223,551; and the total prison population was 643,371, or 274 per 100,000. I was also frightened by this enormous prison population, particularly by its growth up to 1983, and put the article aside to write about it. But these figures and the comments were soon to be outdated.

Diagram 7.2-1 shows what has later happened. It gives the number of prisoners in Federal and State institutions from 1925 to 1998. I have extended the line up to the year 2005, as it will look if the recent development continues. Jails are not included in this Figure. I have placed a small vertical mark on the line at the point where the experts revealed their concern. From that time and up to 1998, the prison population in the USA has tripled.

Another picture of the growth can be read out of the figures we presented earlier, in *Table 3.4-1*. We estimated there that the one-year growth in the prison population from 1998 to 1999 was 109,170 new prisoners. This growth is so great that it is difficult for Europeans to grasp its meaning. Denmark, Finland, Norway and Sweden have altogether 14,066 prisoners. The US figures for one year of growth are close to eight times as large as the total prison population in Scandinavia. But even compared with the United Kingdom, the US figures are remarkable. The total prison population in the UK in October 1998 was 73,545, which means that the USA in one year adds more prisoners to its prison population than all the prisoners in the

Diagram 7.2-1. Sentenced prisoners in State and Federal institutions USA, per 100,000 resident population, 1925–1998. Estimated growth 1999–2005.[1]

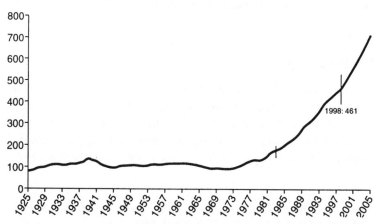

1 Sentenced prisoners in State and Federal institutions on December 31, rate per 100,000 resident population (from Sourcebook of Criminal Justice Statistics 1997, p. 490). The number includes prisoners in custody. Estimates 1999-2005 are based on the average annual increase 1990–98 – 6,5% (Bureau of Justice Statistics, Bulletin, "Prisoners in 1998", p. 2).

United Kingdom. We would have to add to the UK figures the total prison population of Austria, Belgium, The Netherlands and Switzerland to reach the magnitude of one year of growth in the US system.

The size of this growth can be illustrated by the need for new prisons. According to European standards, a prison with 500 inmates is a large prison, many would say much too large. But let us again be conservative and suggest that it would be OK to build new prisons with a capacity for 1,000 prisoners.[1] If this were the norm, the USA would have had to build 83 such prisons last year (1998) to absorb the growth. In the period from 1983 to 1999, they would have needed 1,242 new prisons. No wonder that this is the base for a large industry.

Those who have arrived in Federal or State institutions will mostly stay for a very long time. Nearly all have sentences of one year or more. The average stay for those released in 1994 was 31 months.[2] But not all are released. In 1990, 11,759 inmates were serving what the Americans call "natural life sentences", which means they are sentenced to die in prison. In 1996 their number had increased to 17,280 (*The Corrections Yearbook 1991* and *1996*). There were in 1996 more than 270,000 serving life sentences of 20 years or more. 3,335 were waiting for execution in 1997. From 1977 to 1 January 1999, 500 prisoners were executed. Between 1930 and 1998, 4,359 were executed.[3]

7.3 Black figures

We saw in *Tables 3.4-4* and *3.4-6* that most of those controlled by the penal system were relatively young males. But these young males are of course not selected at random. For the poor city dwellers in the USA, to be a prisoner or probationer, or to be surrounded by such persons, is a natural part of life, particularly if one belongs to the

---

1 According to *The Corrections Yearbook* for 1996, 70 were opened at the Federal and State levels that year, with a capacity of 69,421 "beds".
2 Bureau of Justice Statistics, *Sourcebook 1997*, p. 431.
3 Department of Justice 1999, *Sourcebook on Criminal Justice Statistics*. Online, *Tables 6.75* and *6.88*.

ethnic minorities. Close to half of the prison population in the USA is black. Black males had in 1996 an incarceration rate of 6.6%, or 6,607 per 100,000 adult black males in the population. White males had 944.

Marc Mauer has carried out extensive studies of African Americans and the criminal system (e.g. Mauer and Huling 1995 and Mauer 1999). In the last of these two reports he writes (p. 124):

> Half of the inmates in the nation's prisons were African American, compared to their 13 percent share of the population, and one in fourteen adult black males was locked up in a prison or jail on any given day.

> For young black men, the situation was far worse. A study by The Sentencing Project found in 1989 nearly one in four black males in the age group 20–29 was under some form of criminal justice supervision on any given day – either in prison or jail, or on probation or parole. A follow-up study in 1995 then found that this figure had increased to almost one in three, a remarkable rise over a short period of time. Further, a black boy born in 1991 stood a 29 percent chance of being imprisoned at some point in his life, compared to a 16 percent chance for a Hispanic boy and a 4 percent chance for a white boy.

In the big cities, the situation is even more extreme. Jerome Miller (1996, p. 7) has this to say:

> In 1992, the National Centre on Institutions and Alternative Studies conducted a survey of young African American Males in Washington DC's criminal justice system. It found that on an average day in 1991, more than four in ten (42%) of all the 18–35 year-old African American males who lived in the District of Columbia were in jail, in prison, on probation/parole, out on bond, or being sought on arrest warrants.

> ...it was estimated that approximately 75% of all the 18-year-old African American males in the city could look forward to being arrested and jailed at least once before reaching age 35. The lifetime risk probably hovered somewhere between 80% and 90%.

> ... on an average day in Baltimore, Maryland, 56% of all its young African American males were in prison, jail, on probation/parole, on bail, or being sought on arrest warrants.

With all this in mind, it is easy to understand that Marc Mauer (1991, p. 9) formulates one of his sub-titles in an earlier report like this:

AFRICAN-AMERICAN MALES: AN ENDANGERED SPECIES?

And Mauer continues:

> African American males, who are disproportionately low-income, face a
> variety of problems, including: the social and economic decline of our
> inner cities and diminished opportunities for young people; the continuing
> failure of our schools, health care systems, and other institutional supports
> to prepare young Black males to occupy legitimate roles in society; contin-
> uing poverty and a distribution of wealth which has resulted in even greater
> disparity between the rich and the poor over the past twenty years.

And this over-representation of blacks is steadily increasing. Austin
and McVey (1989, p. 5) point to the war against drugs as one important
explanation:

> Drug enforcement has been narrowly focused on crack, the drug of choice
> among the underclass, which is also disproportionately Black and
> Hispanic. Consequently, the proportion of offenders sentenced to prison
> who are non-white is escalating.

Mauer agrees:

> From 1984 to 1988, the Black community's percentage of all drug arrests
> nationally increased from 30 percent to 38 percent. In Michigan, drug
> arrests overall have doubled since 1985, while drug arrests of Blacks have
> tripled. With a "war on drugs" primarily waged through the criminal
> justice system and disproportionately targeting inner-city users, the end
> result is an increasing number of prisoners and an ever larger share of
> Black inmates.

Florida is probably the most extreme among states in this regard. In
1982/1983, there were 299 felony drug cases brought against male
juveniles in Florida. There were 54 cases against black juveniles. In
1985, the number for whites was 336, while the blacks had now – with
a figure of 371 – overtaken the whites. But then, in 1989/90, the
number for blacks had increased to 3415, while whites were lagging
far behind with only 526.[4] The architect behind this growth, Governor
Martinez, lost the election for a new period as Governor, but has
instead become the drug-tzar for the whole country.

4 From the Florida Supreme Court Racial and Ethnic Bias Commission, 1991.

It does not seem unreasonable to think that the combination of being black and poor is a handicap at the court-level as well, although this is debated (cf. the discussion between Wilbanks and Mann, 1987). Personally, I have never been able to forget the results of a little study by Wolfgang, Kelly and Nolde as far back as 1962. They compared prisoners admitted to death row. In all probability, black people came into this queue with greater ease – that means for reasons somewhat less sound – than white people. As a result, one might have expected that a relatively smaller quota of black people would eventually be executed after having gone through the various appeal procedures. But the results were the opposite. Relatively more blacks than whites were executed. Mauer's last book (1999) gives several examples of general mechanisms working against blacks in the legal process.

It is an ironic situation. Slavery was abolished. The African Americans were free to move. So they do – and end in prisons. In that very moment, they also lose their political power. According to Fellner and Mauer (1998, p. 2) an estimated 3.9 million adults in the USA have currently or permanently lost the ability to vote because of a felony conviction. 1.4 million among them are African American men. That is 13 percent of the black adult male population. In seven states one in four black men is permanently disenfranchised. Given the current rates of incarceration, three in ten of the next generation of black men will be disenfranchised at some point in their lifetime. In states with the most restrictive voting laws, 40 percent of African American men are likely to be permanently disenfranchised. Fellner and Mauer (p. 6) also describe how easy it is to lose the right to vote, and the difficulties in getting the right back:

> Most state disenfranchisement laws provide that conviction of any felony or crime that is punishable with imprisonment is a basis for losing the right to vote. The crime need not have any connection to electoral processes, nor need it be classified as notably serious. Shoplifting or possession of a modest amount of marijuana could suffice.
> ...
> In at least sixteen states, federal offenders cannot use the state procedure for restoring their civil rights. The only method provided by federal law for restoring voting rights to ex-offenders is a presidential pardon.

***

But do not let us believe that these differences are unique to the USA. In all industrialized countries, socially deprived minorities are over-represented within prisons. European prisons have also darkened. If poverty had colour, they would have darkened even more. There is no reason for European chauvinism vis-à-vis the USA. Langan and Farrington (1998, p. 44) compare the situation in England and Wales with the United States in 1991: In the USA at that time, 2563 per 100,000 of the black population and 396 per 100,000 of the white were incarcerated. In England and Wales 667 blacks per 100,000 and 102 per 100,000 of the whites were incarcerated. That means in both countries six times as many blacks as whites. It is the size of the problem that makes the USA situation unique.

7.4 From state to state

Of all the beautiful states, California is probably number one. Here is sun, here is leisure, here is Berkeley and Stanford and the heaven of academic life, here is business and expansion and work, here is Hollywood, the dream-factory of the world.

And here are also some of the more famous prisons in the United States. Alcatraz is gone, but San Quentin remains with a fame stretching far beyond the USA. And here is Folsom with 7,000 prisoners, 500 among them probably never to be released. And in these years, new structures are being added to the great Californian tradition.

In 1977, California had 80 prisoners per 100,000 in Federal and State institutions sentenced to one year or more. In 1998, the relative figure was 483, or 158,742 persons. The head of the California Correctional Peace Officers Association (CCPOA) has a solution. He wants the state to build mega-prisons, each for 20,000 inmates. A few mega-prisons, he says, could satisfy California's demand for new cells into the next century.[5]

Diagram 7.4-1 takes us from state to state. The figures show the number sentenced to more than one year in Federal and State institu-

5 Schlosser (1998), p. 76.

Diagram 7.4-1. Prison figures per 100,000 inhabitants 1998 in the US sentenced to more than 1 year in Federal and State Institutions.[1]

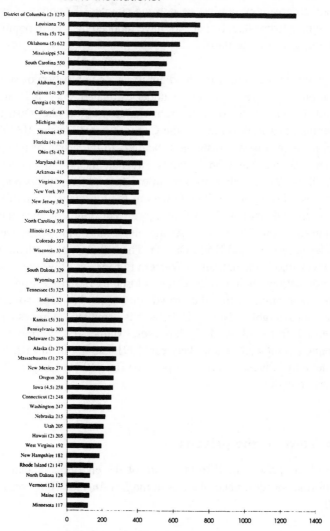

1 Source: Bureau of Justice Statistics. Bulletin. "Prisoners 1998", p.3.
2 Prisons and jails form an integrated system. Original data includes total jail and prison population. The original figures are reduced by 1/3.
3 The incarceration rate includes an estimated 6,200 inmates sentenced to more than 1 year but held in local jails or houses of correction.
4 Population figures are based on custody counts.
5 "Sentenced to more than 1 year" includes some inmates "sentenced to 1 year or less".

tions per 100,000 inhabitants in each state. Nearly all their prisoners have such long sentences. Jails are not included here. This means that one-third of the US prison population is excluded. Some states have an integrated prison system where jails are counted. To obtain comparative figures from state to state, we have reduced the prison population in these states by one-third.

The major impression from the diagram is a combination of size and variation. The size is of course under-estimated since jails are not included. But even so, it is remarkable to find the District of Columbia, that is Washington, the Capital, with 1275 per 100,000 of its citizens in prison. Washington belongs to the group of integrated systems, so we can with certainty say that their total number per 100,000 is 1913, or close to 2 %. In our first edition of this book the figure was 1186 per 100,000. Others in the top range are Louisiana, Texas and Oklahoma. Texas has more than doubled since the last edition, up from 297 to 724. At the other end of the scale, we find Minnesota, Maine and North Dakota. These figures bring them to the top-level among the nations of Western Europe, but if we then add the jail population, their profile comes closer to Eastern Europe. Also worth mentioning is that the growth in the number of prisoners has been considerable. North Dakota has doubled, Minnesota has increased from 78 to 117; however, Maine and Vermont have remained completely stable between 1991 and 1998, in fact, Maine has actually reduced its prison population from 127 to 125 per 100,000 of its population.

7.5 State of the prisons

One of the prisons built to take care of the enormous expansion in California was described like this in the *Los Angeles Times* on 1 May 1990:

> Pelican Bay is entirely automated and designed so that inmates have virtually no face-to-face contact with guards or other inmates. For 22 1/2 hours a day, inmates are confined to their windowless cells, built of solid blocks of concrete and stainless steel so that they won't have access to materials they could fashion into weapons. They don't work in prison industries; they don't have access to recreation; they don't mingle with other inmates.

They aren't even allowed to smoke because matches are considered a security risk. Inmates eat all meals in their cells and leave only for brief showers and 90 minutes of daily exercise. They shower alone and exercise alone in miniature yards of barren patches of cement enclosed by 20 feet high cement walls covered with metal screens. The doors to their cells are opened and closed electronically by a guard in a control booth.

...

There are virtually no bars in the facility; the cell doors are made of perforated sheets of stainless steel with slots for food trays. Nor are there guards with keys on their belts walking the tiers. Instead, the guards are locked away in glass-enclosed control booths and communicate with prisoners through a speaker system.

...

The SHU (Secure Housing Unit) has its own infirmary; its own law library (where prisoners are kept in secure rooms and slipped law books through slots); and its own room for parole hearings. Inmates can spend years without stepping outside the Unit.

According to *Corrections Digest* (27 June 1990, p. 9), the Governor of California had this to say at the opening:

"California now possesses a state-of-the-art prison that will serve as a model for the rest of the nation. ... Pelican Bay symbolises our philosophy that the best way to reduce crime is to put convicted criminals behind bars."

The Governor also noted that the annual cost of keeping a convicted felon in prison is 20,000 dollars compared with the 430,000 dollars that it costs society when a career criminal is at work on the street.

California is not alone. From Oklahoma, *The Sunday Oklahoma* of 24 February 1991 had this to report:

Inmates housed in the "high-max" security unit will live 23 hours a day in their cells, with the other hour spent in a small concrete recreation area with 200-foot walls. The space is topped by a metal grate. Theoretically, an inmate could move into the new cell house and never again set foot outdoors. The unit's first residents will be the 114 men on death row. The cell house also contains a new execution chamber.

The organization Human Rights Watch has investigated prison conditions in the USA. This study is a parallel study to the one by Helsinki Watch on prison conditions in the Soviet Union. In a detailed report (1992), Human Rights Watch describes trends towards total isolation in the US prisons. They call the trend "Marionization". A federal prison with that name implemented a series of extraordinary security measures in 1983, and most states have followed suit in creating their own super maximum security institutions called "Maxi-Maxi" in prison jargon.

> The confinement in "maxi-maxis" is administered by prison officials without independent supervision and leads to a situation in which inmates may in fact be sentenced twice: once by the court, to a certain period of imprisonment; and the second time by the prison administration, to particularly harsh conditions.
>
> The conditions at Marion are much harsher than in any other federal prison, including confinement of inmates for up to 23 hours a day to their cells and denial of any contact visits (p. 4).

State prisons have the same arrangements. From Florida, this is reported:

> A particularly glaring example is the windowless Q-Wing of the Florida State Prison at Starke, from which inmates *never* go outside and where some prisoners have been held as long as seven years (p. 4).
>
> ...
>
> Such a placement is open-ended, and may last, we were informed, for as long as 15 years. The inmate is allowed three showers and two hours of outdoor exercise a week as the only time outside the cell. He can buy a limited number of goods from the canteen and check out one book a week from the library (if he is not on the Library Suspension List, another disciplinary measure at Starke). Inmates under close management can also be deprived of all exercise outside the cell and not allowed outdoors for years at a time. The Florida rules claim that "Close Management is not disciplinary in nature and inmates in close management are not being punished." (p. 44)

Disciplinary confinement is even more serious, meant for prisoners who commit an infraction within the prison. In addition to the restrictions associated with close management, these inmates are not allowed any reading material except legal materials. But life can turn even worse. This prison has a Q-Wing for those who commit further infractions while already in one of the categories described above. Cells are here 6 feet 11 inches by 8 feet 7 inches, with a cement bunk, a toilet and a sink. There is no window and no furniture. The door is of metal. The heat in the cell was stifling, according to the Human Rights Watch (p. 45).

Another construction was launched in 1997. *Correctional Digest* (5 December 1997) has this description:

> Designers were able to cram everything a prisoner needs into a 105 square foot cell. Each will hold two prisoners in bunk beds and will have a toilet, sink and shower. And for the first time, the cells also will have doors leading outside to very small – about 6 by 8 feet – enclosed balconies where prisoners will take their daily one hour of exercise time.
>
> The doors to the exercise areas will be controlled electronically by officers in a central control room, so they can decide when prisoners can go in and out.
>
> The metal door of each cell that opens to the inside corridor of the prison won't allow prisoners to communicate between cells. Smaller doors within each door will allow officers to pass in food and to shackle prisoners before opening the cell door.
>
> The state plans to hire 19 additional officers and two sergeants to work at each of the new facilities. Officials say that's adequate to supervise 200 prisoners in this new environment, which was devised to avoid prisoner officer contact.

"Cold Storage" is the title Human Rights Watch (1997) put on one of its publications – and on all these special institutions (p. 18):

> Thirty-six states and the Federal Government currently operate a total of at least fifty-seven super-maximum security units, called "supermaxes", built either as annexes within existing prisons or as free-standing facilities. Construction under way will increase nationwide supermax capacity by nearly 25 percent.

The same report quotes Federal District Judge Thelton Henderson's observation (p. 10):

> Sedating all inmates with a powerful medication that leaves them in a continual stupor would arguably reduce security risks; however, such a condition of confinement would clearly fail constitutional muster.

According to available statistics, it appears that 1.8% of all sentenced prisoners in the United States are now held in maximum security, including what is called "supermax". The equivalent proportion in the United Kingdom is 0.1% (Coyle 2000). But again the USA is a land of contrast. Extreme isolation is one type of evil. But the extreme contrast to isolation also has its costs. The Human Rights Watch (1992) also describes these conditions (pp. 19–20):

> Jails are supposed to hold inmates for briefer periods than prisons, and that fact is reflected in the physical structure of most institutions. They often have very limited recreation facilities, house inmates in windowless cells, and provide little or no privacy to the detainees.

> For example, the Criminal Justice Centre in Nashville, Tennessee was built in 1982 with a capacity for about 300 inmates. At the time of our visit in 1990, it held more than 800 inmates and we were told that at some point recently it had held 1,100. For over six months, a staff member told us, the facility's gym was used to house several hundred pre-trial detainees. They had two bathrooms and two showers at the gym. At the time of the greatest overcrowding, additional space in the underground tunnel leading to the courthouse was used to house 200 inmates. There were no showers and no bathrooms in that area.

> ... on Rikers Island in New York City, out of 1,516 inmates at the time of our visit about 300 were housed in cells (mostly segregation) while the rest lived in dormitories and on the decks of converted ferry boats anchored to the shore of the island. Each dormitory housed up to 57 inmates.

> ... In the Sybil Brand jail in Los Angeles, women slept in dormitories holding between 130-156 people. The dorms were crowded and offered no personal privacy.

The complaints from these prisoners were strikingly similar to those we have quoted earlier from Russian prisoners. But this is from USA:

> Dormitories were designed for 50, yet held about 90 inmates at the time of our visit. Inmates complained to us about the crowded conditions and about not being able to choose a roommate. A severely overweight woman (she told us her weight was 280 pounds) said that when she and her roommate were both in the cubicle, they literally could not move (p. 34).

> One inmate ... described his cell (in another prison): "Peeling paint on walls, leaking plumbing, broken glass in windows, dim lighting, roaches, rats/mice, ants, mosquitoes, mouldy pillows and mattress, covered with filth, which have no plastic covers, unbearable heat in the summer, intense cold in winter."

But the USA is a country of contrasts, in other directions as well. Again, according to the Human Rights Watch (p. 61):

> Among institutions visited by Human Rights Watch, only the Bedford Hills facility allowed inmates who gave birth during incarceration to keep their babies in prison. Under a New York State law, female inmates are allowed to keep their babies for one year.

> In addition to accommodations for babies, Bedford Hills, a facility where 75 percent of the inmates are mothers, has arrangements to help them maintain contacts with older children. In the summer, the facility runs week-long programs for inmates' children who are housed with local families and spend the day with their mothers on the premises. They play with their mothers in a large, toy-filled visiting room, and may also participate in a number of organized activities. In addition, they can also use a playground outside. Year-round, according to the warden, there are bus rides once a month from New York City and Albany, arranged so that children can visit their mothers without having to be accompanied by other relatives.

7.6 The crime explanation

The conventional explanation for the growth in prison rates is to see it as a reflection of the growth in crime. The criminal starts it all, and society has to react. This is re-active thinking. As we have already commented, this thinking does not hold up for Europe. And it fares no better in the USA.

In 1990, the prison population had doubled during the previous ten years. But here is what the Bureau of Justice Statistics said (*National Update*, January 1992, p. 5) about the number of victims in that period:

> Victimization rates continue a downward trend that began a decade ago.

> There were approximately 34.4 million personal and household crimes in 1990, compared with 41.4 million in 1981.

> From 1973 to 1990, the rate of personal crimes (rape, robbery, assault, personal theft) fell by 24.5% and the rate for household crimes (burglary, household theft, motor vehicle theft) fell by 26.1%.

> Because the NCVS (The National Crime Victimization Survey) counts only crimes for which the victim can be interviewed, homicides are not counted. Their exclusion does not substantially alter the overall estimates.

Furthermore, and again in sharp contrast to folk-beliefs on crime in the USA, the number of serious offences reported to the police also showed a slight decrease. The FBI statistics on serious offences started at 5.1 million in 1980 and ended at 4.8 million in 1989. But the severity of the sanctions for these crimes had increased. In 1980, 196 offenders were sentenced to prison for every 1,000 arrests for serious crimes. In 1990, the number of sentenced for such crimes had increased to 332, according to the Bureau of Justice Statistics on Prisoners in 1990.

Mauer (1991, p. 7) had these comments:

> While there is little question that the United States has a high rate of crime, there is much evidence that the increase in the number of people behind bars in recent years is a consequence of harsher criminal justice policies of the past decade, rather than a direct consequence of rising crime.

The United States differs from most industrialized countries when it comes to murder. Compared to England and Wales, the country has at least six times as many murders. Compared to Scandinavia, it has ten times as many. But even in the USA, murder is a rare act, and the difference here cannot at all explain the enormous difference in prison populations between the USA and Western Europe. And certainly, murder can not explain the increase in the prison population. *Diagram 7.6-1* illustrates the United States Murder Rate 1960–97. We find no dramatic increase after 1975. But the figures are high. And when it comes to other crimes, the USA is not so different from other countries. A picture of this can be found in the study by Langan and Farrington (1998) where they compare crime and justice in the United States with England and Wales in 1981–96. A basic impression from their study is the similarity between the two countries on such indicators as self-reported crimes, reporting to the police, and clearance rates. But the US police record more of what is reported to them; offenders there are more often *sentenced* to imprisonment, and the sentences are more severe.

Diagram 7.6-1. United States murder rate per 100,000
inhabitants, 1960–1997

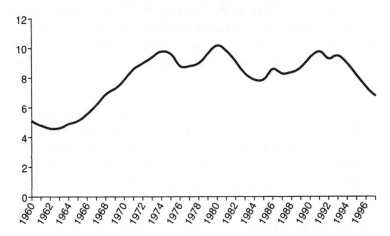

The explosion in the number of prisoners in the USA cannot be explained as "caused by crime". It has to do with penal policy. The Bureau of Justice Statistics *Bulletin* gives this overview, August 1999:

> Factors underlying the growth in the State prison population between 1990 and 1997 included:
> – a 39% rise in the number of parole violators returned to prison and a 4% increase in new court commitments
> – a drop in annual release rates of inmates from 37% in 1990 to 31% in 1997
> – an increase in the average time served in prison by released inmates (from 22 months in 1990 to 27 months in 1997) and the time expected to be served by those entering prison (from 38 months to 43 months)
> – a small but growing number (10%) of inmates who will serve 20 or more years in prison before release and 5% who will never be released.

It is particularly those prisoners sentenced for violence who will be kept longer in prison. The tendencies described above will automatically lead to a greater percentage of persons sentenced for violence in US prisons, but this increase is a result of administrative and judicial decisions, not of the "crime situation". But even this increase has not been very great. The number of violent offenders in the State prisons has risen from 46% to 47% from 1990 to 1997, while the drug offenders went down from 22% to 21%. But in jails, violence cases went down from 30% to 26% and drugs up from 9% to 22%. This was for the period 1983 to 1996. In the Federal prisons, as we already documented in Chapter 5.3, drugs are totally dominant. In 1970, when the Federal system held 20,686 sentenced prisoners, 16% were there for drugs. In 1997 it held 90,992 – but at that time 60% of these were for drugs.[6]

Instead of looking at prison as an answer to crime, one might turn it upside down and look at social phenomena as an answer to prison conditions. Children are sent to business school to learn. From teachers, from fellow students. And they will gain friends and colleagues – for life. Prisons are no different, and they have their own curriculum. Schlosser (1998) says:

> The lesson being taught in most American prisons – where violence, extortion, and rape have long been routine – is that the strong will always rule the weak. Inmates who display the slightest hint of vulnerability quickly become prey. During the 1950s and 1960s prison gangs were formed in California and Illinois as a means of self-protection. Those gangs have now spread nationwide. ... Many of the customs, slang, and tattoos long associated with prison gangs have become fashionable among young people. In cities throughout America, the culture of the prisons is rapidly becoming the culture of the streets.

This was already visible some years back:

> Richard Stratton, editor of *Prison Life* magazine, thinks there's a growing interest in prison culture in general, and that prison fashion is a part of that. ... "What you're seeing is the prison culture spilling out and becoming the general culture," he says.

> The current style of baggy, ill-fitting clothes started in prison. The reason: Belts are taken away from inmates so they're not used as a weapon or to commit suicide. So low-riding pants are a prison tradition. Stratton says rap music and the tattoo fad also originated in prison. "That's all prison culture that moved out into the culture at large." *USA TODAY*, 2 November 1995.

6 Bureau of Justice Statistics, Sourcebook 1997, Table 6.52.

7.7 The brakes are gone

Understanding social life is to a large extent a struggle to find out what sort of meaning the phenomena are given – and why. Are kings the sons of God, or descendants of particularly successful criminals? And the beautiful people, at the top of business or entertainment, are they there due to virtues comparable to their life-styles? Are poor people to be seen as idle drinkers, good-for-nothing, or as victims of social conditions outside of their control? Are inner cities places where those with no aspirations choose to flock together, or are they dumping grounds for those not given an even share of the benefits of modern societies?

Inner cities are filled with deplorable acts – wife-abuse, selling of sex, selling of crack, killings. Acts seen as crimes. Crimes seen as targets for war. But again, these phenomena could, in addition and at the same time, have been given alternative meanings. They might first and foremost have been seen as indicators of misery, demands for economic, educational, and treatment facilities on a scale comparable to what is invested in wars outside the national border. The fascinating question, seen from an outsider's perspective, is why the inner cities of the USA are seen as targets for war rather than as targets for drastic social reform.

As early as 1831, Alexis de Tocqueville (here 1990) observed that the democratic spirit and struggle for equality he met during his travels in the USA at that time, also had some potential problematic aspects. Particularly he feared the potential tyranny of all this equality (1990, p. 231):

> For myself, if I feel the hand of power heavy on my brow, I am little concerned to know who it is that oppresses me; I am no better inclined to pass my head under the yoke because a million men hold it for me.

And he states, regarding the judiciary (p. 131):

> My greatest complaint against democratic government as organized in the United States is not, as many Europeans make out, its weakness, but rather its irresistible strength. What I find most repulsive in America is not the extreme freedom reigning there but the shortage of guarantees against tyranny.

When a man or a party suffers an injustice in the United States, to whom can he turn? To public opinion? That is what forms the majority. To the legislative body? It represents the majority and obeys it blindly. To the executive power? It is appointed by the majority and serves as its passive instrument. To the police? They are nothing but the majority under arms. A jury? The jury is the majority vested with the right to pronounce judgement; even the judges in certain states are elected by the majority. So, however iniquitous or unreasonable the measure which hurts you, you must submit.

Some will say, this can not continue. It will be too expensive and therefore have to come to a stop.

I doubt it. Who considers money in the middle of a war? The war on drugs, the war on violence, the war on pornography – the urgent need for safe streets and property, these are archetype situations where money is not allowed to reign.

The particular danger in this situation is that developments in the USA might reinforce what happens in Russia, and vice versa. Opponents to the explosion in the number of prisoners in one of the big nations are easily muted by reference to what goes on in the other. Criticism directed towards the increasing number of prisoners in Russia can easily be met with a "look to America", and in the USA, the knowledge of prison figures in Russia might also comfort the conscience.

This mutual encouragement created between the two former world leaders, might also have consequences for the remaining industrialized world. When the USA breaks away from all earlier standards by what she does against parts of her population, and when Russia regresses to her former standards, then a threat is created against what is usually seen as an acceptable number of prisoners across the industrialized world. A new frame of reference is established. As a result, Western Europe might have increasing difficulty in preserving its relatively humane penal policies. The other countries in Eastern Europe might also feel encouraged to follow the examples from the two world leaders in incarceration.

Chapter 8

Crime control as a product

Usually we think of crime control as something outside money and market conditions. The solemn judges in their robes, and even more the system of penal measures, are far removed from market conditions. Punishment is a state obligation, a burden forced on us if we want to remain as ordered societies; it is an activity outside trade, money and profit.

This chapter presents another view. It looks at the penal system as highly influenced by market conditions. Pain delivery is an activity of great economic importance for the providers.

In what follows, I will first describe the pain-market in the way that market expresses itself in its specialised business journals – the publications for staff and entrepreneurs in the prison industry. Thereafter, I will develop three major themes which explain some of the growth in the system: the private push, the technological push, and lastly, the importance of the prison industry in the national economy.

8.1 The self-presentation

From the folklore, we know that everything is bigger in the USA than everywhere else. Nonetheless, to a foreigner, it is a moving experience to have in the hand the official publication of the American Correctional Association. The title is *Corrections Today*, a magazine with glossy pages, in colour and perfect print, containing a mass of advertisements which are probably a considerable source of income to the Association. More in the form of a newspaper, but also with glossy pages is *Correctional Building News,* which appeared in 1994. It presents itself as a newsletter for "The Correctional Building Industry", and is packed with advertisements from builders and producers. In 1999 it changed its name to *Correctional News.* The editor explains (July/August p. 6): "This means expanded coverage, as is evident here in our first 48-page issue ever. Now, facility managers and service providers can expect to find more news coverage than ever about services contracts, and more features about management issues affecting jails, prison and detention centres."

The issue for June 1991 of *Corrections Today* contained 111 advertisements. It was my first meeting with the journal, and it made such a great impression that I made a rough estimate of the contents of these advertisements that month, as well as of some from the following issues. I am a regular reader of the journal. The trend seems to be the same over the years, so my rough estimate in 1991 is still valid. Three major categories were heavily represented in the advertisements:

1. Building of prisons, entire prisons, or parts of prisons. There were sixteen such ads. You phone and we build. Six months after your call, the prison is ready. Besteel is one of those. In a full page ad we are told:

> Albany County Jail and Penitentiary. 64 bed dormitory style Jail (...) Completed in 6 months.

Bell Construction also has a full page under the title:

The Pros on Cons

> For more than 20 years we've been building. Building a reputation. Building a client list, and building correctional facilities. That's all we do, we build. ... And we do it well. Twenty-five correctional facilities worth $300 millions have given us the experience, and now our clients call us the "pros".

> Are you building or renovating a correctional facility? Are you interested in a design-built facility at a guaranteed price? If you're interested in finding out more about our experience, call Don Estes, senior vice president at ...

Some authorities may be in need of a site for their prisons. The Bibby Line group has a solution according to the ancient tradition of the ship of fools:

Maritime Correctional Facilities

> Times change. ... Bibby OFFERS alternatives to land based facilities. Bibby DELIVERS:
> – Crisis relief within 90-120 days
> – Up to 650 beds within 9–12 months

2. Equipment for prisons. In this area, the June issue contained 43 ads of all sorts. Among them were three for telephones particularly suitable for prisons, twenty for electronic surveillance systems of all sorts, three for weapons and seven for other security equipment.

Phones that enforce

This is a whole page ad by USWEST Communication:

> This phone only does what *you* want it to do. It controls how long callers talk. It bars them from reaching certain numbers. It can monitor and record all phone activity, as directed. ... Keep inmate telephone privileges firmly under your control ...

Or:

> Designed for Criminal Justice Professionals: Drug Abuse? Yes or no in 3 minutes. ... Rapid results leave no time for alibis. ... ONTRAK allows no time for excuses and gives you complete control of the testing situation.

"Prison Band"

> Identify inmates with a heavy duty waterproof wristband. Two locking metal snaps ensure a non-transferable heavy duty no-stretch identification system. No special tools are needed to close our metal snaps. Both write on surface and insert card systems are available. SECUR-BAND, the answer for inmate identification.

The issue of *Corrections Today* for June carried an enormous number of advertisements, but that issue was soon to be dwarfed. In July the number of pages increased from 160 to 256. Ordinary ads increased from 111 to 130. Partly, they were of the same types as in June, like the one for tear gas:

> The TG Guard system, now installed in major prisons, is a strategic arrangement of tear gas dispensers installed at the ceiling level. These dispensers can be fired from a remote-control console by protected personnel. The firing can be in a chosen pattern and with various levels of concentration to force the inmates to evacuate an area in a route which you determine.

If tear gas is not sufficient, Point Blank Body Armour is available:

> Some inmates would *love* to stab, slash, pound, punch and burn you. But they won't get past your S.T.A.R. Special Tactical Anti-Riot vest.

In addition to the usual ads, the July issue also contained sixty yellow pages called:

Buyer's Guide of Correctional Products and Services.

Here were listed 269 companies, with a specification of their products, from A – Access Control Systems, via P – Portable Jail Cells, down to X for X-ray and security screening equipment. The list shows the latest in electronics, but also firms with traditions, like the:

Human Restraint Company

> Finest quality leather restraints. Manufactured in USA since 1876. Call or write for a free brochure.

This official publication of the American Correctional Association does not only contain paid advertisements, it also carries articles, squeezed in between the ads. But several of the articles are written by employees of the very same firms which advertise in the journal. The July issue has an article by Rohn and Ostroski, both from Precision Dynamics Corporation, a manufacturer of identification systems. Here is what they tell us from Los Angeles, which has, in their own words, the largest single detention facility "in the free world". In this extraordinary place, they have trusted inmate identification wristbands for almost 14 years. But Georgia has a more sophisticated system:

The crowded DeKalb County Jail near Atlanta, Ga. houses more than 1,200 inmates. In the winter of 1989, officials there decided to begin using bar code wristbands that employ the same basic technology as bar codes used in clothing stores and supermarkets.

...

To create a rehabilitative atmosphere – and still maintain a high security level – jail officials installed a laser-scanning and portable data-collection system to identify and monitor the inmates.

By using hand-held laser units to scan the wristbands, deputies enter data into a small computer. This method of gathering information eliminates the paperwork involved in monitoring inmate movements.

...

Technology is now being developed to allow inmate photos to appear on the same wristband as the bar-coded information. ... Inmates can't switch bands, which prevents erroneous releases. (pp. 142–145)

Two pictures illustrate the article. Both show black arms – nothing more – with wristbands controlled by white arms in one picture, and by the whole of a white person in the second picture. It is probably not possible to get much closer to a situation where humans are handled as commodities – based on a technology so well-known from the supermarkets.

3. The running of prisons also plays a prominent part, with twenty ads in the June issue:

"When morale's on the line with every meal, count on us. ... Service America is working behind bars all across the country, with a solid record of good behavior ... If feeding a captive audience is part of your job, talk to the food service specialists who know how to do justice. Call ..."

Another condition for peace is efficient weapons. Efficient firms provide non-lethal as well as lethal weapons. Among the non-lethal:

Cap-Stun II

Used by the FBI and 1100 Law Enforcement agencies
Never a law suit involving Cap-Stun in 14 years of use
Proven effective against Drug Abusers and Psychotics
Consumer models available for friends and loved ones

Among the 111 advertisements in June, there were also a few for ordinary products for ordinary people, not particularly relevant to the prison markets.

The July issue also contains two other extraordinary items. One consists of several pages of thanks to the sponsors of the banquet to be held at the annual Congress of Correction in Minneapolis. From telephone companies to manufacturers of bullet-proof glass, they pay, and the prison officers celebrate. An additional attractive feature of the congress is that you can leave the town "in a beautiful, sporty, brand-spanking-new 1991 Dodge Daytona ES fully equipped with every imaginable accessory!" The only condition is that you visit the Exhibit Hall where the industry shows its products, and get proof that you have been there. When you are registered in the Hall, you are automatically a participant in the lottery for the car.

***

One personal note on the adaptability of man: On my first reading of *Corrections Today*, I was close to not trusting my own eyes. The image of the prisoners that emerged through the ads was close to unbelievable. So was also the frank exposure of the relationship between the correctional establishment and the industrial interests. Medical journals are of course similar, and pharmaceutical firms excel in their briberies of doctors through sponsorship of their congresses, seminars, trips to Hawaii with spouses included and all that. But doctors are supposed to be of some benefit to their patients. The American Correctional Association is of another kind. It is the organisation with a mandate to administer the ultimate power of society. It is an organisation for the delivery of pain, here sponsored for eating, drinking and dancing by those who make the tools.

But then, to continue my personal note: the next shock came some weeks later, when I re-read the journals. Now the ads no longer had quite the same punch. I saw advertisements for gas dispensers in the ceiling of prisons without immediately connecting the picture or the text to old images of extermination camps, and I read without great excitement about inmates who would love to stab, slash, pound, punch and burn me and other readers. I had got accustomed to it, domesticated to a highly peculiar perspective on fellow beings, and I had also acquired new (reduced) minimum standards for what sort of surroundings some people can decide that other people have to live in.

8.2 The private push

Prison means money. Big money. Big in building, big in providing equipment. And big in running. In May 1994, the American Jail Association arranged a training conference in Indianapolis. The industry received this invitation as a preparation for the conference:

JAIL EXPO 1994

TAP INTO THE SIXTY-FIVE BILLION DOLLAR LOCAL JAILS MARKET

Jail Expo attendees are the decision-makers in local corrections – sheriffs, jail administrators, local elected officials, correctional officers, health care directors, food service directors, trainers, architects, engineers – people from across the nation involved in jail management issues, new trends, services, and products.

There are over *100,000* people who work in the nearly 3,400 local jails in the United States. Last year alone over *$65 BILLION* was spent in the industry. The local jail market is very lucrative! Jails are BIG BUSINESS. (The emphasis is not mine).

According to Knepper and Lilly (1991), health care and food service were two of the fastest growing sectors in the booming corrections industry. But the biggest profits are made in construction and finance (p. 5):

The average costs of a U.S. prison bed in 1991–1992 is $53,100, up from $42,000 in 1987-1988. Not surprisingly, more than a hundred firms specialize in prison architecture alone, and these firms now receive between $4 billion and $6 billion in prison construction business a year.

A natural consequence of this building boom was the appearance in 1994 of *Correctional Building News.* A recurrent theme here is this:

> Inmates are built tougher
> than ever before
> Fortunately, so is our furniture.
>
> XX furniture is manufactured
> to be virtually indestructible.
> No wonder we get so much respect in prison.

Or, as the text across a huge picture of three men looking extremely dangerous:

> Before we introduced
> our new Hi. Impact Wallboard,
> we ran it by a few experts.

And we are assured that the product:

> will stand up to whatever they throw at it.

Or this adaptation to the sentencing terminology from Y-enterprises:

> Everything you'll need for
> the next 20 years to life.

Builders are happy. But so is also the stock market. Corrections Corporation of America and their competitor Wackenhut are some of the most promising investment-objects on the USA market, according to the *Wall Street Journal*, 10 April, 1996. A stock-broker upgraded his advice regarding Wackenhut from "buy" to "strong buy", and explains:

> The beauty of the prison-management business ... is that incarceration rates are increasing faster than the prison budgets of many states and municipalities. Though the savings are difficult to measure, analysts contend that Wackenhut typically can slash 15% from the $50 it takes government to clothe, feed and guard an inmate each day.
>
> "It's a win-win situation," says Mr. Ruttenbur, explaining that both taxpayers and prison companies benefit.

He says nothing about where the loss can be found.

***

Privatisation is nothing new. It all started with privatisation, first in England and later in the USA. Prosecution was private, the police were private, local prisons were private – run by alehouse-keepers. Most importantly, transportation was a result of private initiative and business instincts. The result was that some 50,000 convicts were shipped across the Atlantic. In the words of Feeley (1991a, p. 3):

> Shortly after the first colonists arrived in Virginia in 1607, they were fol-
> lowed by a handful of convicted felons transported there as a condition of
> pardon to be sold into servitude. Thus was set into motion a new penal
> system, a system that operated successfully for nearly 250 years ...

> ... transportation to the New World was a marriage of efficiency and effec-
> tiveness. Most of its costs were borne by profit-seeking merchants selling
> their human cargo and by planters who purchased it. It was effective in that
> it sanctioned thousands of offenders who otherwise would have gone
> unpunished.

> ... transportation was an innovation promoted by mercantile interests which
> was only reluctantly embraced by public officials as they slowly came to
> appreciate its cost effectiveness.

> ... The policy of transportation multiplied the states penal capacity and at
> low cost to the government. It expanded the reach and efficacy of the crim-
> inal sanction without the need for a centralized bureaucracy.

And the tradition of privatisation was directly carried over into the prison system. When transportation came to an end, some of the surplus ships were placed in San Francisco Bay. Maritime Correctional Facilities as advertised by the Bibby Line group have a long history. In San Francisco Bay, they housed convicts while they built the prison at San Quentin. The many famous early prisons built in the USA were also dependent on money from the private contractors who used convict labour. Several large prisons were leased to private contractors.

> The size of the prison population was determined not by the amount of
> crime or the need for social control or the efficiency of the police, but by
> the desire to make crime pay – for government and private employees.

It is Novak (1982) who says this, here quoted by Ericson, McMahon and Evans (1987, p. 358) in an article with the telling title "Punishing for profit". And they continue:

> The Mississippi prison system celebrated the fact that it turned a profit every year until the Second World War. It was only in the late 1920s and into the 1930s that legislation extinguished the convict lease system, apparently in response to pressure from rural manufacturers and labor unions who could not stand the competition, especially with the coming of the Depression.

Even the central idea of how prisons ought to be shaped was formulated by persons who wanted to create prisons for profit. It is well-known that Jeremy Bentham designed the Panopticon, the building which so to speak symbolises total control. "Pan opticon" means total view. Bentham's invention is built as a huge shell in a circle with a tall tower in the middle. In the external circle are the cells. They have windows facing both in and out. In the tower in the middle are the guards. From their position they can see through every cell and observe everything without being seen themselves. It provided for maximum surveillance at a minimum cost. Jeremy Bentham also planned tubes so the sounds from each cell could be monitored.

Bentham designed and developed plans for private contractors to run his institution. What is more, according to Feeley (1991a pp. 4–5), Bentham "campaigned tirelessly to obtain this contract for himself, believing that it would make him a wealthy man. From the early 1780s until the early 1800s, he was obsessed with this idea. He invested thousands of pounds of his own money in efforts to acquire a site and to develop a prototype of the Panopticon."

He lost his investment. But his basic design became influential, both architecturally and economically.

The private prison as we know it today does not represent any continuation of the old idea of galley slaves and workhouses. The model is instead the old one with municipal care for the poor. Auctions were often arranged. Those who had the lowest bid got the goods – the care of the poor. Possibilities for profit in running poor houses is a debated topic. But with the large-scale arrangements now growing up, no doubt remains. Here it is a question of big money. And, most important, with this amount of interplay with private profit interests, even up to the level of private prisons, we are building a growth factor into the system. The central question is, as stated by Feeley (1991a, p. 2) *to what extent does privatisation expand and transform the state's capacity to punish?*

Logan's (1990) view is that privatisation will not necessarily lead to increased capacity of the prisons:

> On the whole, however, businesses succeed not by stimulating spurious demand, but by accurately anticipating both the nature and the level of real demand (p. 159).

And how then to decide what the "real demand" is? Logan has an answer:

> ... prison flow should respond to the crime rate, which is largely beyond the control of the state; therefore, prison capacity must be flexible (p. 170).

Right now, there is – according to Logan – a genuine unmet demand for imprisonment (p. 161). And this is worse than oversupply:

> If both oversupply and undersupply can lead to injustice, we should, in principle, err on the side of oversupply, although this is not likely to happen for some time to come (pp. 151–152).

With a view on crime as an unlimited natural resource for the crime control industry, we see the dangers in this type of reasoning. The economic interests of the industry, with confirmation from Logan, will all the time be on the side of oversupply, both of police and of prison capacity. This establishes an extraordinary strong incentive for the expansion of the system.

In addition comes the fact that privatisation makes it simple both to build and to run prisons. Advocates of private prisons are in trouble here. It is difficult both to argue for the speed, flexibility and economic advantages of privately run prisons, and at the same time claim that these advantages will not lead to an oversupply. Logan describes the advantages (p. 79):

Private companies have demonstrated repeatedly that they can locate, finance, design, and construct prisons more rapidly than the government can. Corrections Corporation of America reports its construction costs to be about 80 percent of what the government pays for construction. CCA notes that it can build not only faster, thereby saving inflation costs, but also at a lower immediate cost, since construction contractors charge the government more.

Private financing also makes for a simpler life for government. It is not necessary to ask the voters for permission to build new prisons, the government can instead rent prisons from private industry, or borrow money from it for the construction. In Logan's words, "... it avoids the cost of a referendum" (p. 79). It also makes it simpler to run the prisons since strikes of the employees can more easily be prevented:

> Since a strike or other disruption would allow the government to terminate a contract, unemployment as the result of a strike will be a credible threat to private officers. In contrast, such threats do not often deter strikes in the public sector.

As a help, also to the public sector, Logan suggests:

> ... to couple legislation requiring that all correctional officers – public and private – be certified, with legislation providing for automatic de-certification of officers who participate in a strike.

With private prisons as the extreme example, but also with the economic/industrial establishment as providers of services to prisons run by the public, a highly efficient growth factor is built into the system. Just as we illustrated from *Corrections Today*, interested sellers line up, their tools for the efficient delivery of suffering are displayed, and the prospective buyers are bribed to come and see. When the government is also given help both to avoid their voters and to prevent strikes among the staff, highly efficient mechanisms for expansion are created. Lotke (1996, p. 21) express the fears among many when he states:

> In coming years, as the private prison companies expand their operations, the prison-industrial complex's influence over criminal justice policy is likely to grow significantly. Criminal justice policy may someday be as influenced by Corrections Corporation of America as defence policy is influenced by Lockheed Martin and McDonnell Douglas.

***

One problem might remain, but the industry has its solution: The building-boom might go too far, some states might be left with empty prisons. In such situations, private firms turn to "bed brokers" for help, to recruit prisoners from out of state. Eric Schlosser describes the mechanism (1998, pp. 65–66):

> By the mid-1990s, thousands of inmates from across the United States were being transported from overcrowded prison systems to "rent-a-cell" facilities in small Texas towns. ...
>
> The private-prison industry usually charges its customers a daily rate for each inmate; the success or failure of a private prison is determined by the number of "man-days" it can generate. In a typical rent-a-cell arrangement a state with a surplus of inmates will contact a well-established bed broker. ... The broker will search for a facility with empty beds at the right price. The cost per man-day can range from $25 to $60, depending on the kind of facility and its level of occupancy. ... Bed brokers earn a commission of 2.50 to 5.50 per man-day.

In 1987, there were 3,000 prisoners in institutions run by private firms. In 1996, there were 85,000.[1] During the next decade, the number of private prison beds in the USA is expected to soar to 360,000, says *USA TODAY*, 5 June 1996. And it relates further:

> Investors who own stock in Wackenhut Corrections have learned that their mothers were wrong: Crime pays.
> Shares of the private prison manager have soared 203% this year. Tuesday, the stock hit a 52-week high.
> ...
> Behind Tuesday's move:
> First, the company said it won a $49 million contract to operate a 200-bed detention center for the Immigration and Naturalization Service.
> ...
> Later, the Virginia Department of Correction said it selected Wackenhut to build and operate a 1,000-bed prison.

---

1 National Institute of Justice, April 1999. Examination of Privatization in the Federal Bureau of Prisons. Solicitation.

8.3 The technology push

With the end of the cold war, the military-industrial complex was in trouble. But this situation did not last long. A new enemy emerged: the enemy at home. In 1993, a seminar was held at Johns Hopkins University. The theme was "Non-lethal defence". Janet Reno, Attorney General of the United States, was presented with a message at the opening of the seminar.[2] In her formulation:

> While you – Defense, the Intelligence communities and the industrial sector – were winning the cold war for the nation, we were slowly losing the war against crime here at home. In the five years that ended with the collapse of the Soviet Union, crime in the United States increased more than 30%.

> So let me welcome you to the kind of war our police fight every day. And let me challenge you to turn your skills that served us so well in the cold war to helping us with the war we're now fighting daily in the streets of our towns and cities across the nation.

And the Attorney General ends with these words:

> We have a wonderful opportunity to capture the fruits of all your labors through the cold war. If we can capture some of what you've already done and find ways to adapt it to our peacetime problems together, we can take back the streets of America for the sake of our children and those who follow.

> Won't you please join us in this very crucial crusade?

The themes for the conference were these:

- Increase Awareness of Law Enforcement Requirements
- Increase Understanding of the Value of Technology Applied to Law Enforcement
- Highlight Technology Transfer Opportunities for the Defence Industrial Base
- Emphasize Opportunities for Industry in the Law Enforcement Market Place

---

2 Delivered on the Attorney General's behalf by David G. Boyd, Director of Science and Technology, National Institute of Justice.

A year later, in 1994, a second conference took place, this time called "Law Enforcement Technology for the 21st Century". This time the opening statement came from William H. Webster, former Director of the FBI, later Director of CIA. His opening words:

> As Conference Chairman, I want to welcome those of you from law enforcement, criminal justice, industry, defense, technology and public policy communities.
>
> ...
>
> A partnership of the U.S. Departments of Justice and Defense and industry is critical in addressing the needs of law enforcement research and development. I am glad to see these partners together at one event, and I want to express my gratitude to the sponsors of such an event who are making technology available to those who do 95 percent of the community policing – State and local law enforcement agencies.

And who were these sponsors? They were listed in the daily newsletter from the conference as this:

> While this conference has many supporters, the primary sponsor is the NIJ (National Institute of Justice), with major support from the American Defense Preparedness Association (ADPA) and the International Society for Optical Engineering (SPIE).
>
> ...
>
> SPIE is a nonprofit technical society dedicated to advancing engineering and scientific applications of optical, electro-optical, and opto-electronic technologies through its publications, symposia, and short courses. SPIE brings the latest technological breakthroughs to the doorstep of individuals and organizations all over the world by facilitating interaction between those with the information and those who want it.

This co-operation between the military establishment and the establishment of law and order would be beneficial to both parties. Morrison (1994, p. 891) quotes Anita K. Jones, Pentagon Director of Defense Research and Engineering, in a statement to U.S. politicians:

> There is a very important military motivation for our alliance with (Justice). ... With the passing of the cold war era, the U.S. Armed Forces are increasingly being given missions that are quite different from the traditional wars of attrition and destruction.
>
> Military rules of engagement for (peacekeeping and humanitarian relief missions) place severe limitations on casualties and collateral damage in

military operations, often resulting in the same set of options afforded to the policeman.

And what do they learn at their conferences?[3] They learn of course that they are at war, the enemy is everywhere, dangerous, mobile. He has to be fought by military measures, captured, put in prison, and thereafter followed step by step if he ever comes out. These are golden days for the electronic industry. In a beautiful pamphlet from one of the conferences, we get a presentation of the Remote Consultation Information Systems. Here is the text:

> Technology description: The Constant Watch is a stainless steel wristwatch or bracelet affixed and locked to a parolee's ankle. A Global Positioning System chip in the Constant Watch bracelet will track the individual's changing location and transmit the data back to the police station via the Broadband Code Division Multiple Access (B-CDMA) communications technology, using the existing cellular and Personal Communication Systems (PCS) infrastructure already available.

> Technology Impact: How do we keep track of potentially dangerous parolees and repeat offenders? If a parolee moves out of the prescribed freedom area or removes the Constant Watch bracelet, the Constant Watch computer system will immediately alert police officers who can take corrective action to contain the offender. Keeping accurate track of individuals who are released from prison, due to prison overcrowding for example, will improve the odds for law-abiding citizens who unknowingly run the risk of injury or death at the hands of freed career criminals.

> There are currently over two million adults either on probation or on parole in this country. Just think about the task of tracking, locating and controlling the movements of these individuals. Then think of how the accomplishment of that task would be enhanced and simplified with the Constant Watch bracelet permanently attached to them during their probation or parole periods.

The system of electronic bracelets is being improved all the time. On 2 May, 1996 *Business Wire* reports that public safety is taking a giant

---

3 New conferences follow all the time. I cannot keep track of them all, here in my Norwegian periphery. The most recent on my desk is an invitation from The National Institute of Justice in 1996, with the support of the American Defense Preparedness Association. Under the heading "An Excellent Opportunity to Participate in a Growing Market", participants were invited to a plenary session followed by "a technology reception among the displays in the exhibit hall".

leap forward that same day with the introduction of a device that tracks and continuously monitors offenders and stalkers, and provides advance warning for victims:

> A loud sound can be instantly sent to the offenders, warning them if they stray into a prohibited zone. For example, sex offenders are often ordered by the courts to stay away from schools and playgrounds. Any violation would trigger an alarm and notify the appropriate agency.
>
> ...
>
> Authorities can program SMART to alert a victim if a stalker is nearby in violation of a court order. The victim's device is equipped with a panic button feature. When depressed, a distress signal is instantly sent to the monitoring center displaying the victim's position.

> "We feel SMART is a significant milestone for our criminal justice system," said former U.S. Drug Czar and former Florida Governor Bob Martinez, president of PRO TECH Monitoring Inc.

The bracelet technology is a complicated one, probably expensive and therefore limited to the more serious cases. 'Ameritech' is a cheaper system, but seems to have a solution for everybody in this market of four million people on probation and parole. It is a system of voice verification for monitoring offenders on minimum supervision or administrative probation. This service accepts calls from offenders under minimum supervision, positively identifies the individual using voice verification, and identifies the location using the telephone number from which the offender is calling.[4]

Satellites and telephones can control where the parolees are. But the penal law system might also need to know details of their condition. Mitsubishi was one of the first companies to offer help. Their system was specifically designed for "home prisons"[5], but can of course also be used for probationers everywhere.

---

4 *Corrections Digest,* 9 August, 1996, p. 5.

5 In the home prison the prisoner gets an electronic device around his wrist and ankle. The bracelet is connected to the telephone. If the home prisoner leaves the house, the connection to the telephone is broken, and an alarm sounds in the police or probation headquarters.

In a full-page ad in *Corrections Today* of June 1991, we are shown a whole control package. It contains the usual electronic bracelet, but in addition there is a telephone combined with a television transmitter and a device for testing the blood alcohol level. Soon, I feel sure, televised urinating will also be added. Here is an excerpt of what Mitsubishi describes:

> To meet the growing needs in home detention, a monitoring system must be versatile, reliable, and capable of checking alcohol usage. The risk is too high to settle for less.
> ...
> The system automatically calls the client (up to four at a time), requests some action (in any language), and records the picture with time, date, and name (providing hard evidence).
> ...
> When it comes to Breath Alcohol Testing (BAT), only MEMS provides remote, unassisted, positive visual proof of a client's blood alcohol level and his identity. And, it's all done automatically from the computer base station.

But up to now, "old" technology is still dominating the market for controlling people on parole and probation. Old technology means ordinary drug testing and guns.

First to the guns: In California, as in several other states, the weapon industry got probation-workers, those who earlier perceived themselves as social workers, as their new customers. Probation in California was in danger of losing ground – and jobs. To survive, probation officers had to choose sides – between being social workers without jobs, or crime controllers. They chose the latter alternative in a move which illustrates so much of what Stan Cohen (1985) has discussed as role-blurring. In this case, their move was symbolised by giving the parole officers guns as equipment. Smith (1991, p. 124) writes:

> We selected the Smith & Wesson Model 64, 38-calibre revolver. It is relatively lightweight, stainless steel, with a two inch barrel. It carries six rounds and is easy to conceal under the clothes agents normally wear. We chose ammunition that had the maximum stopping power without fragmenting.

And then the drugs. According to Messinger (Messinger and Berecochea, 1991):

> ... something like 400,000 drug tests were done last year on parolees here. I think that's one heck of a lot of urine that has to be taken.

What has happened is that early release is being followed by tight control, and now that the technology is there, it is eagerly used. At intervals, released prisoners are forced to pee. They belong to the segment of the population where drug use is part of the life-style. Before, while probation was still social work, they might have received mild warnings, and hopefully some help to survive. Now a technique exists for their control, and back they go. It is a beautiful example of the management of the dangerous classes. Now it is not necessarily the original crime which brings them back to prison; it might be aspects of their life-style. Control of drugs means control of the lower classes.

Guns and drug testing seem to be the major reasons for the extraordinary growth in the prison figures for California already from 1980 to 1990. Those years were affluent years. Frank Zimring (1991, p. 22) has a diagram for the period showing the rate of unemployment in California moving dramatically downwards, as the rate of imprisonment ascends straight to heaven. Messinger relates this directly to the combination of guns and tests: Prisoners are released on probation. And probation has totally changed its character: "... return to prison has become not a rarity but the most common experience for prisoners."

In addition to those returned to prison because of drug use under parole, comes those sentenced directly for drug offences. Together these two categories make up a majority of the prison population. In 1986 they were 30 per cent, in 1988 35 per cent, and in 1991, 53 per cent of the prison population.

This policy is under continuous development. According to a report from U.S. Department of Justice (Henry and Clark 1999), President Bill Clinton in 1995 directed Attorney General Janet Renot to develop and implement a universal policy providing for the drug testing of all federal arrestees before the decision is made to release them to the community pending trial. He also directed the Attorney General to take steps to encourage states to adopt and implement the policy.

Henry and Clark report on the various methods in use. The ease and simplicity of this technique is particularly illustrated in what they describe as HAND-HELD URINE TESTING. Most of these devices are similar in appearance, about the size and shape of a credit card. A result is obtained by depositing drops of urine into a sample well. The results appear within minutes, usually indicated by a coloured line. Several of these devices test for a single drug, whereas others test for multiple drugs simultaneously.

> Hand-held devices have become very popular with criminal justice agencies due to their portability, ability to rapidly provide results, and ease of operation. Because they require no machinery to maintain and calibrate, they can be used by criminal justice officers with no formal training in drug testing.

But there are also other technical advances. One is a device for testing perspiration. It is done like this:

> The PharmChek sweat patch is an adhesive patch attached to the skin, usually on the upper arm, of a testing subject. The patch, which can remain on the skin for up to one week, is tamper evident, meaning that any effort by the subject to remove it is obvious. As the subject perspires, the sweat is collected by a pad, which is then tested at the vendor's laboratory ...

Hair analysis is a third method. Because drugs are absorbed into hair shafts, a history of drug use is produced as each hair strand grows. The only limit on the length of time in which drug use can be detected is the length of the hair – one inch of hair can track any drug use over a 60-day period. But it is an expensive method and a difficult one to use on individuals with very short hair, according to Henry and Clark (p. 5).

This trend to go after the drug-users is also, as documented earlier, clearly visible in European welfare states. Everywhere in modern states, drugs become the major form of deviance used as a lever in the control of those at the bottom of society. With a little help from the drug-testing industry, these possibilities are close to unlimited.

***

Technology is also increasing its efficiency inside the prisons. In addition to the many ads quoted earlier, let me bring this article from *Correctional News*, July/August 1999:

> SAN FRANCISCO – A variety of high-tech tools and non-lethal weapons to control unruly inmates are under scrutiny by the California Department of Corrections. Correctional officers are already outnumbered seven to one by convicts. With the state's inmate population of 160,000 estimated to rise 19 percent to about 191,000 in the next five years, the new tools are sorely needed to run smarter and safer prisons.
>
> One such device is the TSI Prism system, a computerized inmate tracking and alarm system similar to ones used by the military. Every two seconds, the system updates the location of inmates, who wear wrist-watch size devices that emit wireless signals. These signals are collected by receivers, travel along a cable system and are displayed on computers in a prison control room. The signal can transmit when immersed in water.
>
> Correctional officers wear pager size units on their belts, which automatically sound an alarm if they fall or are forced into a horizontal position.
>
> Guns that fire non-lethal ammunition, including a hard sponge device used by U.S. forces in Bosnia and Somalia, are other options. Various pepper spray devices that can be worn on belts, deployed from fire extinguishers, sprayed from water pistols or used to douse inmates up to 150 feet away are also available.

A particularly helpful tool for prisons stems from the television industry. I do not have in mind the usual TV-programs run to pacify the prison population. When an execution is to take place in a prison, it is seen as essential to have a good film on the prison circuit. What I have in mind are the new possibilities in Video Conferencing and in Telemedicine. Transporting a prisoner is a heavy strain on any system. It increases the risks of escape, it requires equipment and personnel, time and money. The Video Conferencing can limit the movement of inmates and still permit them to have arraignment, parole or probation hearings without leaving the facility, writes *Corrections Forums*, January 1996. And continues (p. 24):

Through the use of these video systems inmates can have their day in court, a parole hearing or other interaction and never leave the facility or even their own cell.

...

Lincoln Hill chose to solve the problem with a video conferencing system that permitted the creation of a "virtual courtroom" presence in Lincoln Hill so juveniles could make their courtroom appearances without ever having to leave the facility.

...

Its newest innovation is MultiView 5 plus 1. All participants appear simultaneously on a video monitor divided into six sections. The highlight screen, or largest of the six, is voice activated and displays whoever is speaking. The five surrounding images let you see all the other parties at once, all the time.

With all the preparation and expense required for transporting detainees or inmates, systems like these hold great promise in the area of reducing costs, saving travel time and expense, and increasing security.

Cameras can be installed in holding areas, jails, detention centers, courtrooms, even a judge's chambers.

Prisoners can also get sick. Again the problems of transport, security and costs arise. And again technology offers new opportunities, this time under the name of Telemedicine. The National Institute of Justice has a report on the possibilities in 1999. The heading sums it up: *Telemedicine Can Reduce Correctional Health Care Costs.* According to the summary in the *Corrections Digest*,[6] prisons that utilise telemedicine systems, instead of the conventional prison health care, could save labour costs of $102 per patient encounter. And *Corrections Forums* (January 1996, p. 26) explicates:

Because most facilities are built in unpopulated and isolated areas, medical professionals, inmates and the personnel required to escort them, must often travel great distances to receive care beyond the infirmary level.

...

An additional feature available from some telemedicine health care providers, like Wexford, is mental health and chemical dependency components that can be used to treat disturbed or addicted inmates.

The joint consequences of these technical innovations is increased

6 28 May, 1999, p. 1.

capacity at all levels. Surveillance of the prisoner is increased, knowledge of his body while on probation is increased, opportunities for the return to prison are increased, and when the prisoner is behind walls, the video-technology lets him remain there, both during court proceedings and sickness. A picture of him, or parts of him, might appear in the court or in the hospital. But what we are accustomed to think of as the subject, the person in all its complexities, the full human being, that subject remains behind walls, or is only presented as a voice, as a picture or as a chemical test. If it is true, and it is, that physical and social distance makes it is easier to carry out unpleasant measures against other human beings, then recent developments in electronics have created ideal conditions.

8.4 Prisons as units for production

Prisons and prisoners are not always quite the strain on the economy as one might expect. Concentration camps and GULAGS are relevant examples. And modern times have their own examples.

First, the building of new prisons can be made inexpensive because the builders are supposed to suffer. They can be forced into long hours and discomfort because the intention is punishment. Texas illustrates the point. The Executive Director of their prison system delivered, in January 1996, "An Overview of ... their Growth and Changes". He describes the expansion:

> What has happened to the Texas prison system in the past 10 years is absolutely mind-boggling. In 10 years we have gone from 37,000 prisoners to soon-to-be 145,000, a quadrupling of the system, an increase of 108,000 inmates, the increase alone larger than any other total prison system in America except California.
>
> ...
>
> In the end, our expansion was accomplished at one-half the national average prison construction cost! Even though we used private contractors, we accomplished that record by using prototype prison designs instead of re-inventing the wheel with a new architect on every unit and by using many inside components such as all the fabricated steel made inexpensively in our prison industries by unpaid inmate labour.

In other words, the one prison produces modules for new prisons, which produce modules for further prisons – and so it can continue until Texas is filled, as it actually became during these years.

The Executive Director continues his report with these points:

- Every inmate in our system has an assigned job and works a full shift every day unless he is on sick call or in transit. No other state can say that.
- Not one prisoner is paid for working. No other can say that.
- We start morning wake-ups as early as 3:30 a.m.
- We expect all prisoners to be on their jobs as early as 5:30 a.m.
- All prisoners wear white uniforms which we make in the prison industries and all prisoners have short hair cuts and clean shaves. No other prison system requires that.
- We have more than 40 prison industries, ranging from a tire recapping plant to garment factories ... and yes, we still make license plates but we also make all the highway signs you see on Texas roadways.

And then:

- Prison management will become a tougher job every day from now on with inmates sentenced to longer and longer minimum terms. There is little incentive for good behavior from an offender who is 32 years old and looking at 40 hard years and knowing he would be 72 years old if in fact he lives through it and finally gets out.

And he ends:

It is both challenge and opportunity on a grand scale.

***

In addition to the low cost of building prisons comes the direct income from prison labour. Prisoners are engaged for federal and state authorities, making furniture, road signs, etc.

Corrections Digest has this headline on October 14, 1999: Prison Workers: Big Businesses Want them, Small Businesses and Unions Fear Squeeze. And they tell:

Federal Prison Industries, Inc. (FPI), a subsidiary of the U.S. Justice Department, last year reported $540 million in sales to its only customers, federal agencies. Today prisoners serving in 94 prisons around the country make electronic components, furniture and camouflage clothing among other things. Now FPI wants to expand into the private sector.

State prisoners are already working for private industry. More than thirty states have made this legal. Some of their products are very popular. *USA TODAY* reports 2 November, 1995 that:

> Prison garb is an increasingly popular fashion item and nothing is hipper than the outfits worn by inmates breaking rocks on the new Alabama chain gang.
> ...
> Convicts at an Oregon state prison have sold their own line of designer prison clothes since 1990. ... Advertising slogans include: "Made on the inside to be worn on the outside".

Compared to doing nothing, working in the prison industry can be seen as a privilege. But it can also be seen as a harsh form of slave labour. That is the perspective of Evans and Goldberg (1999):

> An American worker who once upon a time made $8/hour, loses his job when the company relocates to Thailand where workers are paid only $2/day. Unemployed, and alienated from a society indifferent to his needs, he becomes involved in the drug economy or some other outlawed means of survival. He is arrested, put in prison, and put to work. His new salary: 22 cents/hour.
>
> From worker, to unemployed, to criminal, to convict laborer, the cycle has come full circle. And the only victor is big business.
>
> For private business, prison labor is like a pot of gold. No strikes. No union organizing. No unemployment insurance or workers' compensation to pay. No language problem, as in a foreign country. New leviathan prisons are being built with thousands of eerie acres of factories inside the walls. Prisoners do data entry for Chevron, make telephone reservations for TWA, raise hogs, shovel manure, make circuit boards, limousines, waterbeds, and lingerie for Victoria's Secret. All at a fraction of the cost of "free labor".
> ...
> And, more and more, prisons are charging inmates for basic necessities from medical care, to toilet paper, to the use of the law library. Many states

are now charging "room and board". Berks County jail in Pennsylvania is charging inmates $10 per day to be there. California has similar legislation pending. So, while government cannot (yet) actually require inmates to work at private industry jobs for less than minimum wage, they are forced to by necessity.

8.5 An incentive for rural growth

More important than what the prisons produce is what they consume. By that consumption, they help to keep the country going. This is particularly so because of the prison industry incentives to districts in economic decline. In the old days, nobody wanted a prison in their valley, in their district. Prisons were places of shame. The stigma might spread to their places of living.

Today, this has all changed. There is fierce competition to get prisons in one's district. Politicians and officials are lobbying to get these wonderful stimulants to the economy. They are providers of labour and incentives. And they are stable providers. If the economy declines nationally, it will grow in institutions which receive those most strongly hit by recessions.

The very same day I wrote this, *Correctional Building News* for May/June 1999 reached my mail-box. And here, as the top-news on page 1, I find:

CORRECTIONS REPLACE COAL IN EASTERN KENTUCKY

LEXINGTON, Ky. If three proposed prison projects come to pass, eastern and south-eastern Kentucky could be home to 10 prisons in 10 different counties.
...
In Kentucky's coal country, prisons have become the cornerstone of an economic renewal meant to offset the decline of coal mining.

Appropriate enough, the site for the federal prison in Martin County is a former strip mine, as is the proposed site in Knott County that may house an 895-bed state prison. In Martin County, the unemployment rate in November was 18 percent.

...
An 895-bed prison would create 300 to 400 jobs.

This practice is nothing new. Lotke (1996 p. 21) describes punishment as a leading rural growth industry. "The 1980s saw so many people dragged in shackles from inner city neighbourhoods to rural prisons that 5 percent of the national increase in rural population between 1980 and 1990 is accounted for by prisoners." To the gain of rural areas, to the gain of private companies, and to the gain of correctional officers. Their Labour Union in California uses its influence to lobby for tougher laws, more prison guards and higher wages and benefits. According to Lotke, the average prison guard in California now earns $10,000 more than the average California school teacher.

Schlosser (1998) reports on the wonderful developments in upstate New York – all the way to the Canadian border. Nearly all new prisons are built up there.

> Prisons are labor-intensive institutions, offering year-round employment. They are recession-proof, usually expanding in size during hard times. And they are nonpolluting – an important consideration in rural areas where other forms of development are often blocked by environmentalists. Prisons have brought a stable, steady income to a region long accustomed to a highly seasonal, uncertain economy. (Schlosser p. 58)

The prison boom in the north of the state has had an enormous effect on the local culture. Just about everyone now seems to have at least one relative who works in corrections. Prison jobs have slowed the exodus from small towns, by allowing young people to remain in their own areas.

There is only one problem: The prisons are built in the north, while nearly all the prisoners are from the south. Roughly 80 percent of the state's inmate population comes from New York City and its suburbs. The effect of this can be seen at Columbus Circle in Manhattan. Every Friday night about 800 people, mostly women and children, almost all of them African Americans or Hispanics, gather here, and board buses for the north. The buses travel through the night and arrive in time for visiting hours on Saturday. When the bus company started in 1973, it carried passengers in a single van. Now it charters thirty-five buses and vans on a typical weekend and a larger number on special occasions, such as Father's Day and Thanksgiving.

8.6 Prisons in the national economy

The right to punish has often been a great privilege. It was a display of power. In addition it was profitable. Punishments were often in the form of fines or confiscation – straight to the vault of the emperor.

What are their gains today?

The political gains are obvious: votes and office, and the display of power.

But in addition there are other possible gains. Gains in the drains. An illustration of this can be seen in *Table 8.6–1*. It shows the Federal and State expenditures on corrections in million dollars from 1980 to 1999. From a beginning of 6.9 billion dollars in 1980, it ends at 55.4 billion as the estimated figure for 1999, that is an eightfold increase over 19 years.

Direct costs for running the prisons are only one element of the total costs. In addition come the police and the judiciary. A rough estimate indicates the costs of police protection in 1999 to be 66 billion, while judicial and legal costs amount to 36 billion, or 102 billion in sum.[7] Some of this money is used for other purposes than crime control, but let us assume that at least half – 51 billion – goes to crime control. This brings the total bill for the States and Federal system up to at least 106 billion dollars.

But the total figure is, of course, even higher, and has been so for a long time. David G. Boyd, Director of Science and Technology, the National Institute of Justice, gave some figures in a speech at the opening of a conference on Law Enforcement Technology for the 21st century in Washington June 1994:

---

7 Bureau of Justice Statistics: *Sourcebook of Criminal Justice Statistics 1997*, p. 3.

Table 8.6-1. Expenditures on corrections in million dollars 1980-1999.[1] Federal and State Governments.

Year	Million dollars
1980	6900
1981	7868
1982	9048
1983	10411
1984	11793
1985	13534
1986	15759
1987	17548
1988	20299
1989	22566
1990	26153
1991	29297
1992	31461
1993	31946
1994	35013
1995	38374
1996	42058
1997	46096
1998	50521
1999	55371

1 Source: Sourcebook of Criminal Justice Statistics 1997 p. 3. The figures from 1993 are increased by the annual growth between 1988-1993 which was 9.6% each year.

Since 1988, investment in law enforcement and the criminal justice system has grown roughly at twice the rate of all other federal spending, until as a nation, we now spend more than $75 billion on private security agencies and untold amounts on often unsuccessful efforts to protect our homes and businesses. (Again, these are very conservative figures. Both *Business Week* and *U.S. News and World Report* recently published far larger numbers.)

This supports an earlier report from the National Institute of Justice, by Cunningham et al. (1991, pp. 1–5) which states:

Private security is now clearly the Nation's primary protective resource, outspending public law enforcement by 73 percent and employing 2½ times the workforce, according to a new National Institute of Justice (NIJ) study of the private security industry. Currently, annual spending for private security is 52 billion, and private security agencies employ 1.5 million persons.

In the report, the annual growth in the private security industry is estimated at 8 %. With this growth, the costs of private security in the year 2000 will be 104 billion.

When this is added to public spending, we reach the figure of 210 billion dollars spent on crime control in the USA. This is an amount beyond this author's comprehension. But we might get an inkling of its meaning by comparing it to the US spending on its military forces. That spending was in 1998 256 billion dollars. In other words: The costs of the war against the enemies within is now approaching the costs against the enemies outside the country. While military spending is going down, the spending on crime is going up. It evens out. This tells us something of importance about the nature of the US economy. David Lapido (1999) has this to say.

> We are often told that the dynamism of the American economy stems from the 'deregulated' state of its labour market and, by implication, the 'non-interventionist' stance of the US government. Nothing could be further from the truth. The American labour market is as regulated (and its government as interventionist) as any of its European counterparts. The difference lies, not in the quantity, but in the kind of regulation practised within the United States.
>
> ...
>
> But if the impact of the military industrial complex on the US labour market is widely recognized amongst economists and other social scientists, the same cannot be said of its prison industrial complex. It is true that dollar expenditure on the defence industry is double the amount spent on the carceral industry. (Lapido limits himself here to public spending. N.C.) On the other hand, the 'people intensive' character of America's criminal justice system means that prison spending has a much more immediate impact on the labour market than its more 'capital intensive' defence expenditure.

This brings us to the other gain of the game: The prison industry is absorbing a large amount of the potential work force in the USA. This can be shown in several ways. *Table 8.6–2* illustrates one attempt. We have here included all prisoners in 1999 as well as those employed in corrections at that time. In addition, we have included half of the

Table 8.6-2. Manpower absorbed in the penal law sector, USA 1999. Minimum figures.

	1999
Prisoners[1]	1,934,532
Employees in corrections[2]	775,947
Police[3]	467,351
Employees in judicial and legal sector[4]	440,315
Employees in private security industry[5]	1,939,868
Total	5,558,013
Per 100,000 population[6]	2036
Per 100,000 civilian labour force[7]	3993

1 See table 3.4-1.
2 Sourcebook of Criminal Justice Statistics 1997 p. 25. The figures from 1993 are increased by the annual growth between 1988-1993 which was 4.8% each year.
3 Source as note 2. The figures from 1993 are increased by the annual growth between 1988-1993 which was 1.3% each year. The figure is reduced by 50% to find the number directly involved in penal law activity. This is a low estimate.
4 Source as note 2. The figures from 1993 are increased by the annual growth between 1988-1993 which was 2.7% each year. The figure is reduced by 50% to find the number directly involved in penal law activity. This is a low estimate.
5 The estimate is based on a study by the National Institute of Justice which indicates that the private security industry is employing 2 1/2 times the workforce employed in corrections (Cunningham et al. 1991 pp.1-5).
6 Based on a population of 273 million in 1999. Source: U.S. Census Bureau.
7 Based on a civilian labour force of 139.2 million in 1999. Source: Bureau of Labour Statistics.

police force and half of those employed in the judicial and legal sector. We have also included the employees in the private security industry. Here we have estimated that they are $2\frac{1}{2}$ times as many as those in correction. This gives us a total of 5.6 million persons. The labour force in the USA was 139.2 million in 1999. This means that the crime control industry absorbs 4 percent of the labour force.

This is a very conservative estimate. We have not included the manpower that builds prisons, equips the prisons, and provides all the necessities for running the prisons. But we can conclude, without any hesitation, that without the crime control industry, the labour statistics from the USA would not give that much of a flattering picture of the labour situation in the country. Altogether, no small gain to the emperors. Economists in the USA express considerable satisfaction pointing to the low unemployment figures – success criteria for the market economy. From a criminological perspective, the success story seems slightly tainted.

Chapter 9

Conflicting values

9.1 Pain delivery for sale?

> Even capital punishment is sometimes administered by private contractors in the United States today.

I find the sentence in the major book on private prisons (Logan, 1990, p. 59). There is just this one sentence on capital punishment, squeezed in between examples of all the other tasks administered by private agents. So, for the rest we are free to use our imaginative powers. And I use mine: private contractors for capital punishment – who are they in modern times, and how do they operate? Do they advertise their service? Is it a private, personally-owned firm, or is it registered on the stock exchange as Pain-Delivery Ltd. Limited liability – limited to what? And what about the equipment needed, chairs, needles, poison? Do they provide for it themselves, or sub-contract? And the training of the staff – do they use the available know-how? Joseph Ingle (personal communication, but see also his book of 1990) has described the phenomenon of the left-leg man – he who, in a team of six, specialises in fastening the strap around the left leg, in contrast to the right-legger. Six specialists, reducing the man to die to six parts of a thing.

Why react like this to killing by private contractors? Those to be executed are certainly sentenced by ordinary courts. It all follows basic rules, and officials of the state will certainly see to it that everything is done as decided by that state. The whole execution may actually be better performed than if the state had fumbled with it. The last meal may be better prepared, the psychiatrists and priest may be top performers in their professions, far beyond the reach of ordinary state budgets, and the killing itself may take place without the embarrassing aborted attempts sometimes reported from the state service. Those to be killed would probably appreciate the private quality.

This is the basic line of reasoning in the book by Logan, the only difference being that he writes about the private prison, not the private execution. His conclusion regarding private prisons is clear. All the state is doing, private enterprise can do better, or equally well:

> Arguments against private prisons vary in soundness and plausibility, but in no area have I found any potential problem with private prisons that is not at least matched by an identical or a closely corresponding problem among prisons that are run by the government... Because they raise no problems that are both unique and insurmountable, private prisons should be allowed to compete (and cooperate) with government agencies so that we can discover how best to run prisons that are safe, secure, humane, efficient, and just (p. 5).

I remain unconvinced, and slightly upset. Why is it, that what is so clear to Logan is so utterly unclear to me? His well-ordered book contains a whole chapter on the propriety of private prisons (pp. 49–75). And he finds it proper:

> Our elected leaders exercise very little direct power; rather, they issue instructions and directives that are carried out by subordinates... However, it is false to assume that the integrity of a chain of civil servants is necessarily superior to a contractual chain.

Behind this reasoning is John Locke, and particularly Robert Nozick in his earlier writings (e.g. 1974). They lead Logan to this statement (p. 52):

> In the classical liberal (or in modern terms, libertarian) tradition on which the American system of government is founded, all rights are individual, not collective. The state is artificial and has no authority, legitimate power, or rights of its own other than those transferred to it by individuals.

With this perspective, I can understand Logan's private killing and wish for the privatisation of pain delivery in general. But it is at the same time an arrangement which easily can develop into a monster, a monster with a soft surface. Robert P. Weiss (1989, p. 38) describes that surface:

> private prison companies ... have dispensed with paramilitary uniforms and ranking; martial vocabulary and regiment, which have characterised the penal profession since the inception of the penitentiary, are no longer employed. Prison companies still want to create the illusion of legitimate authority, but a business-like image is projected instead of a pseudo-official one. At CCA-run facilities, for example, prisoners are not referred to as 'inmates', instead they are called 'residents', and guards are referred to as 'resident supervisors'. Dressed in camel-coloured sweaters that bear a discreet company insignia, private guards are represented as what one might call 'corporate security technicians'.

Logan's state is a contractual state. Private persons elect a representative. The representative hires a firm to deliver punishments. If the firm is bad, a new one is hired. The private guard represents his firm. There is nothing more to represent, the state is an artefact. But this means that the guard is under diminished control.

In the opposite case, where the state exists, the prison officer is my man. I would hold a hand on his key, or on the switch for the electric chair. He might be a bad officer. And I might be bad. Together we made for a bad system, so well-known from the history of punishment. But I would have known I was a responsible part of the arrangement. Chances would also be great that some people in the system were not only bad. They would more easily be personally mobilised. The guard was their guard, their responsibility, not an employee of a branch of General Motors, or Volvo for that matter. The communal character of punishments evaporates in the proposals for private prisons. Since the modern private prison is so much an American invention, it is tempting to ask if they have forgotten their old teacher Charles Horton Cooley (1864–1929) who so clearly saw community as the bed of individuality.

Far back in time, we used to mock – fondly – civil servants as persons with two pots of ink on their desks, one for official and the other for private letters. Those days are gone, but not completely. This can be seen if civil servants are found guilty of some kinds of offences, presenting bills for the same air-travel twice, or whatever. Such abuses are mostly seen as more serious matters than if ordinary, private persons commit them. The civil servant represents more than himself, she or he represents the community, that is me. The servant of the state is thus under greater responsibility and control than those who only serve the private firm. This brings us back to the question of honour. If I live under "communal conditions", politicians are a part of me. But so are also those given the task and symbolic quality of being state servants with the mandate to carry out essential functions. Their failure is my shame, their success and decency my pride.

Perhaps this view is more foreign to a reader in the USA where private interests and the contractual state have a stronger hold, than to a European, where the state has existed, forever. Dahrendorf (1985) describes those unbelievable days in Berlin in 1945, the interval between two regimes, when the Nazi-state collapsed and the USSR took over. Some days without state power, and then back to normal conditions where a state, just a different one, was in command. Perhaps Flemming Balvig (in comments on my manuscript) is right when he says that Europeans to a larger extent regard both national states and national cultures as something that has always existed, something given, while this for Americans, to a somewhat larger extent, is something created by them as individuals. Logan's contractual states might be in harmony with American self-understanding. But these differences are far from clear-cut. Jessica Mitford ends her book like this (1974, p. 297):

> Those of us on the outside do not like to think of wardens and guards as our surrogates. Yet they are, and they are intimately locked in a deadly embrace with their human captives behind the prison walls. By extension so are we.
>
> A terrible double meaning is thus imparted to the original question of human ethics: Am I my brother's keeper?

Maybe the respect for the civil servant is on the decline on both sides of the Atlantic. Historically, the civil servant was the King's man, civil only in contrast to a military servant. With reduced Royal power, he became – in theory – the servant of the state. In that capacity, this servant has a potentiality for tuning in to the whole set of values in a particular society, values expressed by politicians, by the public in general, or by all sorts of experts. Recent developments in Scandinavia give some hope: In a political atmosphere with severe moral panics around crime and with populistic claims for law and order and increased severity of punishments, the civil servants have to a large extent stood up as sober and calming elements. Chiefs of police have pointed out that situations have been under control and that more police would not necessarily be a good idea. Chiefs of prisons have made clear that imprisonment has an abundance of negative effects and ought to be used as the utmost restriction. And together they have reminded politicians and the population that criminals also are to be protected by the laws, that they are humans, and that the principles of human rights also exist for their sake. When the Scandinavian prison populations have remained so low even in modern times, it is, in my opinion, to a considerable extent influenced by the moderating effect of a core of independent civil servants.

9.2 Policing for sale?

A similar line of reasoning as the one on private prisons can be formulated regarding private police. This is what Rosenthal and Hoogenboom do in a report to the Council of Europe (1990, p. 39):

> Imagine that private policemen were to handle matters more efficiently and more effectively than governmental police forces. Imagine, to take it a step further, that private policemen were also to treat people equally and according to each and every standard of equity. Then, in spite of the satisfactory fulfilment of all those extrinsic conditions, this would not be sufficient evidence in favour of private policing. In a continental setting, people may feel better about the state doing the job – irrespective of the relative quality of its performance.

But developments in most industrialised nations reveal no sensitivity to this problem. On the contrary, there is a definite trend towards a large expansion in the sector of private policing. This development raises severe problems. But the similarity to the prison arena is not total, which is exposed through the stimulating writings of Shearing and Stenning (e.g. 1987), and also in an important article by Phillipe

Robert (1989). They begin by considering three major points. First, police have of course evolved from being private to becoming the public instrument of the state. Thus, private police are nothing new. Second, with the development of materially rich, large-scale societies, the ordinary police have no chance whatsoever for clearing up more than a tiny fragment of all the problems brought before them. This is bound to create pressure for alternative solutions. And here comes their third point: Private police are, under normal circumstances, also forced to behave as private persons or organisations tend to. They do not have the penal apparatus at their disposal. They are therefore not particularly oriented towards punishment:

> ... the logic of private security systems is blatantly managerial, concerned with risk management, reducing investment at the least possible cost. Repression is far from being a priority: it is counterproductive to the firm's aims, as well as expensive, since it usually involves the use of public agencies. Prevention, rationalisation and compromise are therefore given top priority. (Robert, p. 111)

This, again, opens up possibilities for more civil solutions to conflicts where otherwise penal law would be seen as the only – and badly – functioning alternative.

Private police are dependent on having the public police available – as a last resource. But it decreases the authority of the private agency to have to turn to the public one. And it is a dangerous strategy. The efficiency of the private police is dependent on the belief held by the public that the ordinary police would give the private agency full support if asked to. Maybe they would not.

While private prisons increase the capacity for incarceration, private police might lead to the reduced use of imprisonment. In this perspective, recent developments are not that unattractive. In the opinion of Shearing and Stenning, the contemporary private police are evidence of the re-emergence of private authorities who sometimes effectively challenge the state's claimed monopoly over the definition of order (1987, p. 13):

> ... what is now known about private policing provides compelling evidence
> ... that what we are witnessing through the growth of private policing is not

merely a reshuffling of responsibility for policing public order but the emergence of privately defined orders, policed by privately employed agents, that are in some cases inconsistent with, or even in conflict with, the public order proclaimed by the state.

But the possible gain of getting control away from the domain of penal law – the dream-situation for the abolitionist thinkers – has to be balanced against the two major defects of the private police: their class bias and their potentialities for abuse in situations of severe political conflict.

The class bias has two sides. Least problematic is the obvious fact that upper-class people will be easily able to buy themselves out of embarrassing situations. This is so also within the ordinary penal system. It is close to obvious that all formal systems of control concentrate attention on those strata of the population at safe distance from the power-holders. Exceptional cases of powerful figures brought before the courts are just that: exceptional. A much more problematic effect of private police, is that they will leave lower class areas and interests unprotected. This is the central message from The New Realists in GB. – with Young and Matthews (1992), Young (1989) and Lea and Young (1984) as some of the major exponents. They are completely right when they say that the labour class, and those below, are particularly menaced by ordinary theft, violence and vandalism. Private police, caring for those able and willing to pay, might reduce the interest among the upper classes in having good, public police, and thus leave the other classes and the inner cities in an even worse situation.

In addition comes the problem of the control of the controllers. How to prevent the private police from becoming even more powerful than the recent public police? How to control that the public police will not hire, formally or informally, some of the private ones to do what the public police are not supposed to do? How to prevent the state-power getting some much wanted help from the private groups not hampered by all those soft-handed judges and lawyers?

If the Gestapo or the KGB had been branches of a private firm, hired by dictators, they might have been equally efficient and ugly in their methods, but they would not to the same extent have intimidated their state regimes. When parts of the crime control system belong to the state, there is at least some hope that those parts will be destroyed when the state is destroyed. Hope, but no certainty, as recent developments in several East European states indicate. But if they are private, they are even more protected when the regime falls. Then they belong to a type of organisation where both transnational and national interests see to it that they are allowed to continue. The Gestapo and the SS troops were eliminated after the Second World War, but the firms that provided the equipment for the camps and received the prisoners as slave labourers, are very much alive in Germany today. So are the universities that received research material from the camps.

Chapter 10

Modernity in decisions

10.1 4,926 applicants

I had some problems the other day, but only small ones. We have a selection committee for applicants to the Faculty of Law at my university. I am a member. Once a year we decide on the major intake of new students. There were 4,926 applicants this summer. 500 were to be admitted. Youth unemployment has put immense pressure on the system of higher education. But for us the task was simple. Most decisions on admissions are made on the basis of grades in high school. The grades are added up into one major figure. Some additional points may be included for various types of work experience. A conscientious and highly efficient secretary prepares it all and ranks the applicants. The committee is left with the task of deciding the cutoff point. All applicants above that point are admitted.

But we have two additional problems. Some applicants ask for extraordinary admission for health and social reasons. Maybe they had a severe illness or a death in the family during their final exams, or maybe they were deaf or blind, confined to wheelchairs, or had severe problems with drugs, crime or general mental instability. We discuss each case, and admit most of them. The faculty has to take its share of those in trouble. But at the same time, and in miniature, we face the general welfare problem: Is it right to make it as easy to enter the university via prison or mental hospital as through hard work and good grades from school? Mostly, we have said yes. Luckily, there have not been many such applicants.

Another category also creates problems, not because of the individual applicants, but because of the type of school they come from. Those schools stubbornly refuse to grade their students according to the official grading scale. They insist that final exams and grades do not tell us enough about the pupils. Instead, each teacher at these schools writes a small essay about every pupil in every subject, and adds to this a detailed evaluation of one major piece of work the pupil has accomplished: a painting, a photo exhibition, an essay on Sartre, a reconstruction of an ancient pair of skis from the valley ...

This is impossible – for the selection committee. We had three applicants from those schools this year. I remember them all, inevitably, they come so close. All of them are from the so-called Waldorf Schools, or Rudolf Steiner schools as they are called in Scandinavia. Pupils there have often had the same teachers for 12 years in school. The teachers know them, perhaps too well. Often they write about their pupils with deep insight, and mostly with love. They have been close to their students, and bring them close to us. It makes the task of decision-makers impossible.

Three applicants without grades. And a few "social cases". These were the applicants I got to know . But there were at least 4,400 other applicants who were not admitted. Young people with all sorts of qualities and all sorts of needs for admission. But their qualifications had been converted into numbers, and their numbers were wrong.

To make matters worse – and this is very relevant to my topic of the potentialities of Modernity, I am – for many reasons of principle – against exams and the grading of pupils. I have been an active member of a Royal Commission which proposed the abolition of grades in our compulsory school system. And even worse, I am also against limited admission to universities and have voted against it several times. But I have lost my cases, and feel obliged to participate in the administrative tasks given me. If I had not done it, someone else would have. Maybe I rescue one or two who otherwise would not be admitted to the holy land.

10.2 Bottlenecks

One reason why justice takes so long is that the courts are overburdened with work and poorly equipped to cope with it. This is common knowledge. Time has somehow passed many courts by. The wigs are mostly gone, but not the slow pace. Typewriters have replaced goose quills, and some courts have computers, but by and large, the courts remain bottlenecks, unable to adapt to demands. In addition, their output does not stand up to quality control. Numerous studies show great disparities in sentencing. The same acts result in months of imprisonment in one district and years in another. This creates extra work for the appeal courts, or injustice if not appealed.

In the USA, this is all now about to be changed. Much has already been done.

In 1984, Congress enacted the Sentencing Reform Act. The basic objective of the Act was to enhance the ability of the criminal justice system to combat crime through an efficient and fair sentencing system. Fair meant particularly less disparity. The same acts were to be met with the same punishments. For that purpose, the reform gave both more and less powers to the courts. It gave more power by abolishing the earlier system of indeterminate sentences and parole boards which decided on releases. Time for release would now be decided by the courts. But it also gave less power, by establishing a system of detailed instructions on the sentence in each individual case.

For that purpose, Congress established the United States Sentencing Commission. This is

> an independent agency in the judicial branch composed of seven voting and two non-voting, ex officio members. Its principal purpose is to establish sentencing policies and practices for the federal criminal justice system that will assure the ends of justice by promulgating detailed guidelines prescribing the appropriate sentences for offenders convicted of federal crimes. (U.S. Sentencing Commission Guidelines 1990, § 1.1)

In a decision (Misretta v. United States) the Supreme Court of the United States upheld the constitutionality of the Sentencing Commission against several challenges, so by now the Commission

Table 10.3-1. Sentencing Table (in months of imprisonment)
Criminal History Category (Criminal History Points)

Offence Level	I (0 or 1)	II (2 or 3)	III (4, 5, 6)	IV (7,8,9)	V (10, 11, 12)	VI (13 or more)
1	0-6	0-6	0-6	0-6	0-6	0-6
2	0-6	0-6	0-6	0-6	0-6	0-6
3	0-6	0-6	0-6	0-6	0-6	0-6
4	0-6	0-6	0-6	2-8	4-10	6-12
5	0-6	0-6	1-7	4-10	6-12	9-15
6	0-6	1-7	2-8	6-12	9-15	12-18
7	1-7	2-8	4-10	8-14	12-18	15-21
8	2-8	4-10	6–2	10-16	15-21	18-24
9	4-10	6-12	8-14	12-18	18-24	21-27
10	6-12	8-14	10-16	15-21	21-27	24-30
11	8-14	10-16	12-18	18-24	24-30	27-33
12	10-16	12-18	15-21	21-27	27-33	30-37
13	12-18	15-21	18-24	24-30	30-37	33-41
14	15-21	18-24	21-27	27-33	33-41	37-46
15	18-24	21-27	24-30	30-37	37-46	41-51
16	21-27	24-30	27-33	33-41	41-51	46-57
17	24-30	27-33	30-37	37-46	46-57	51-63
18	27-33	30-37	33-41	41-51	51-63	57-71
19	30-37	33-41	37-46	46-57	57-71	63-78
20	33-41	37-46	41-51	51-63	63-78	70-87
21	37-46	41-51	46-57	57-71	70-87	77-96
22	41-51	46-57	51-63	63-78	77-96	84-105
23	46-57	51-63	57-71	70-87	84-105	92-115
24	51-63	57-71	63-78	77-96	92-115	100-125
25	57-71	63-78	70-87	84-105	100-125	110-137
26	63-78	70-87	78-97	92-115	110-137	120-150
27	70-87	78-97	87-108	100-125	120-150	130-162
28	78-97	87-108	97-121	110-137	130-162	140-175
29	87-108	97-121	108-135	121-151	140-175	151-188
30	97-121	108-135	121-151	135-168	151-188	168-210
31	108-135	121-151	135-168	151-188	168-210	188-235
32	121-151	135-168	151-188	168-210	188-235	210-262
33	135-168	151-188	168-210	188-235	210-262	235-293
34	151-188	168-210	188-235	210-262	235-293	262-327
35	168-210	188-235	210-262	235-293	262-327	292-365
36	188-235	210-262	235-293	262-327	292-365	324-405
37	210-262	235-293	262-327	292-365	324-405	360-life
38	235-293	262-327	292-365	324-405	360-life	360-life
39	262-327	292-365	324-405	360-life	360-life	360-life
40	292-365	324-405	360-life	360-life	360-lif e	360-life
41	324-405	360-life	360-life	360-life	360-life	360-life
42	360-life	360-life	360-life	360-life	360-life	360-life
43	life	life	life	life	life	life

claims to be the determining factor at the Federal level with regard to penal law in the USA.

10.3 Manuals for decisions on pain

One of the major results of the work of the Sentencing Commission is reproduced in *Table 10.3-1*. This is a so-called Sentencing Table. The basic principle for the use of the table is simple enough. Let us first look at some examples of offence levels, the vertical column on the left. The task of the judge here is to decide the type of crime. The crime may be Aircraft Piracy, or Attempted Aircraft Piracy. The Manual, section 2.14 , is clear.

    a)   Base Offence Level: 38
    b)   If death resulted, increase by 5 levels

If death resulted, the offender ends up with 38 + 5 = 43, which is said to mean "life" in the table.

A more complex case would be Burglary of a Residence. The instructions on this read:

    Burglary of a Residence
    (a)   Base Offence Level: 17
    (b)   Specific Offence Characteristics

    (1)   If the offence involved more than minimal planning, increase by 2 levels.
    (2)   If the loss exceeded $ 2,500, increase the offence level as follows:

Loss (Apply the Greatest)	Increase in Level
(A) $2,500 or less	no increase
(B) More than $2,500	add 1
(C) More than $ 10,000	add 2
(D) More than $50,000	add 3
(E) More than $250,000	add 4

(F)	More than $800,000	add 5
(G)	More than $1,500,000	add 6
(H)	More than $2,500,000	add 7
(I)	More than $5,000,000	add 8

(3) If a firearm, destructive device, or controlled substance was taken, or if the taking of such item was an object of the offence, increase by 1 level.

(4) If a dangerous weapon (including a firearm) was possessed, increase by 2 levels.

As we see, the minimum level of punishment would be 17. In the worst case, the maximum is 30.

By this, half the job is done. The remainder is to determine the Criminal History Category. Section 4.1 in the Manual tells how:

(a) Add 3 points for each prior sentence of imprisonment exceeding one year and one month.

(b) Add 2 points for each prior sentence of imprisonment of at least sixty days not counted in(a).

(c) Add 1 point for each prior sentence not included in (a) or (b), up to a total of 4 points for this item.

(d) Add 2 points if the defendant committed the instant offence while under any criminal justice sentence, including probation, parole, supervised release, imprisonment, work release, or escape status.

(e) Add 2 points if the defendant committed the instant offence less than two years after release from imprisonment on a sentence counted under (a) or (b) or while in imprisonment or escape status on such a sentence. If 2 points are added for item (d), add only 1 point for this item.

The maximum in the sentencing table is 13 points. Four earlier sentences exceeding 13 months of imprisonment, and one minor sentence, produce that result.

With these instructions, we could all do the job.

A burglary took place (level 17), well planned (increase to level 19), and resulted in the loss of more than $ 10,000 (increase to level 21), but no guns or drugs were stolen and firearms were not used, so we end down the vertical scale at offence level 21.

The offender had been sentenced twice before to more than 13 months of imprisonment, so his Criminal History Category along the horizontal scale is 6. We go down from that point until we meet the horizontal line from level 21, and the result is clear: The judge is free to choose a prison sentence of between 46 and 57 months.

A bottleneck has been removed.

10.4 Purified justice

The advantage of such a Manual is its honesty. It makes clear what it includes, but also what has been excluded. Congress has been quite specific in its instructions to the Commission on this point. It:

> requires the Commission to assure that its guide-lines and policy statements reflect the general inappropriateness of considering the defendant's education, vocational skills, employment record, family ties and responsibilities, and community ties in determining whether a term of imprisonment should be imposed or the length of a term of imprisonment. (The Manual, p. 5.35)

I must confess I had to read twice: Inappropriateness? In my tradition I would have expected a requirement to let the Manual reflect the *appropriateness* of considering all those factors. But that is not the case, and the Commission follows this up with specific orders *not* to consider:

> Age.
> Education and Vocational Skills.
> Mental and Emotional Conditions.
> Physical Conditions, Including Drug Dependence and Alcohol Abuse.
> Previous Employment Record.

Family Ties and Responsibilities, and Community Ties.
Race, Sex, National Origin, Creed, Religion and Social Economic Status.
(U.S. Sentencing Commission 1989, pp. 5.35–5.37)

To someone used to the old-fashioned European crime policy tradition, these directives are surprising, to put it mildly. On a kind interpretation, the decision to exclude some of these factors may be thought to reflect an attempt to achieve a different sort of justice. Congress may have feared that those who met the right criteria might receive preferential treatment simply for that reason. Upper-class criminals might point to family and community ties as well as to important responsibilities, and thereby unjustly escape punishments given to persons without those ties and responsibilities.

The person who is rich in money and social ties should not thanks to that good fortune escape the full burden of punishment. Fine. But what about persons without ties and responsibilities and with extremely low social status? By preventing the courts from considering all these factors – so as not to give extra advantages to the already privileged – they at the same time block the possibility to show extra leniency towards the particularly disadvantaged. They eliminate the whole question of social justice. What about the very poor offender, who steals out of hunger, or the lonely person, with no social ties at all? To prevent abuse by the (few) well-off persons, the legislators make it illegal for the justice to take into consideration precisely those factors which most of the prison population have as their common background: poverty and deprivation, the absence of a share in the good life, all those key attributes of the non-productive "dangerous class".

If Congress had wanted to ensure that those who were well off socially and economically would not obtain advantages, it could have solved the problem. It is no more complex to operationalize social factors than to operationalize acts which are interpreted as crimes. Let me help the Commission with the following proposed Offence Level scale:

First some points on *increases:*

Offenders with high education (who therefore ought to have known better),
add 2 points

Offenders with an annual income the last two years over X dollars, add 4 points

Offenders with earlier solid social networks and responsibilities, add 5 points

And then as to *reductions:*

Offenders without the minimum compulsory education, deduct 3 points

Offenders defined as living below the poverty level, deduct 4 points

Offenders with extraordinary traumas in youth and insufficient social backgrounds according to a social investigation, deduct 5 points

The list could have been larger, and the weighting heavier. How much culpability is left in a female beaten and sexually abused by her father from childhood, living in misery and poverty – who then in despair kills that father? Or, not to make it too obvious: what about a case where in addition her mother knew about it all without interfering? What weight as a mitigating circumstance should be given to all this, and maybe in addition to having been brought up in a slum? Might it not happen, that when all mitigating factors were added, some culprits would have to be moved *below* Offence Level 1, so that the judge would be obliged to sentence society to give them compensation? To go deep into these matters would mean destroying crime control as a useful theme in the political debate – for those participating in that debate.

Radzinowicz and Hood (1981) describe the development leading up to this situation. So much of the reform stemmed from honest wishes for reduced use of imprisonment. The influential *Committee for the Study of Incarceration* (von Hirsch 1976) was quite explicit in favour of the imposition of less, not more punishment. To abandon the rehabilitative model without a simultaneous gradation downwards in prison sentences would, according to the committee, be an unthinkable cruelty and a dangerous act. Five years, save for murder, would be the highest penalty. Radzinowicz and Hood also quote (p. 142) former Chief Judge Bazelon (1978):

(He) hits the nail on the head when he castigates the Senate's Bill proposing the establishment of a Commission, on the grounds that under the rhetoric of equality it "envisions the criminal process as a vast engine of social control". As the problem of crime is embedded in the social conditions of a society "so judgements must be made within the rich context of an offender's background". The attempt to "automate" this delicate process "deprives participants, and the public itself, of the information that is essential to our concept of criminal justice".

Reasons for not including social factors in the sentencing table are solidly based in the ideology of *just deserts*. The main content of this idea is that punishments ought to reflect the blameworthiness of criminal acts. And the less social factors are included in the account, the clearer the relation becomes between the concrete act and the punishment. Social factors obfuscate the clear and supposedly justly deserved punishment resulting from the evil act. In the framework of just deserts, this is seen as harmful. The moral scale – and the clarity of the message to the population – is blurred. So is the possibility of preventing injustice, in the sense of different punishments for the same acts. The goal is to prevent inequality, but the social consequences are that other important values are squeezed out of the system of decision. Just deserts become just in one sense, but highly unjust where several values ought to be weighed against each other. Since these other values mostly would have counted to the advantage of the disadvantaged, the limitations in just deserts create – in totality – an extremely unjust system. By virtue of its simplicity, it becomes a most useful theory for fast justice and a depersonalization of the offender during the penal process.

10.5 Offender cooperation

According to the Bill of Rights, all Americans accused of crime have the right to a trial by an impartial jury. In the world of realities, hardly any of the accused use this right. More than 90 per cent – in some jurisdictions as many as 99 per cent – plead guilty. If not, if guilty pleas were reduced by even a small percentage, the whole system of courts in the USA would be completely paralyzed.

But why do they plead guilty?

Because they cannot take the risk of pleading not guilty.

The mechanism to assure this fabulous offender cooperation is called plea bargaining. It is simple enough. The prosecutor believes that he can prove that the supposed offender has committed the acts A, B, C and D. He then promises that he will only charge the supposed offender with acts A and B if *the offender pleads guilty to these acts.*

Americans are in this way not sentenced for what they have done, but for what they have agreed with the prosecutor to reveal in court.

The Sentencing Commission did not like the system, and tried to abolish plea bargaining.[1] But they gave it up, among other things because they did not:

> ... find a practical way to reconcile the need for a fair adjudicating procedure with the need for a speedy sentencing process. (1990 p. 1.5)

So, when a judge uses the sentencing table, the act to be categorized is not what it has been proved that the offender has done, but what the offender and the prosecutor have agreed to say that the offender has done – if he is so kind as to confess and thereby assure a simple and fast session in court.

Langbein (1978) points to two consequences of such a system. First, it concentrates enormous power on the side of the prosecution (p. 18):

> Our formal law of trial envisages a division of responsibility. We expect the prosecutor to make the charging decision, the judge and especially the jury to adjudicate, and the judge to set the sentence. Plea bargaining merges these accusatory, determinative, and sanctional phases of the procedure in the hands of the prosecutor.

1 The Commission writes (1990 p. 1.4 – 1.5):
 One of the most important questions for the Commission to decide was whether to base sentences upon the actual conduct in which the defendant engaged regardless of the charges for which he was indicted or convicted ("real offence" sentencing), or upon the conduct that constitutes the elements of the offence for which the defendant was charged and of which he was convicted ("charge offence" sentencing). A bank robber, for example, might have used a gun, frightened bystanders, taken $50,000, injured a teller, refused to stop when ordered, and raced away damaging property during his escape. A pure real offence system would sentence on the basis of all identifiable conduct. A pure offence system would overlook some of the harms that did not constitute statute elements of the offences of which the defendant was convicted.

Radzinowicz and Hood agree completely (1981, pp. 142-143):

> A drastic restriction of the discretionary powers of the judiciary and its supervision by a commission will reduce the judge's role in the criminal process and increase the power of public prosecutors.

But to become able to force the offender to confess, something terrible has to happen if he does not confess. In Langbein's words (p. 12):

> In twentieth-century America we have duplicated the central experience of medieval European criminal procedure: we have moved from an adjudicatory to a confessionary system. We coerce the accused against whom we find probable cause to confess his guilt. To be sure, our means are much politer; we use no rack, no thumb-screw, no Spanish boot to mash his legs. But like the Europeans of distant centuries who did employ those machines, we make it terribly costly for an accused to claim his right to the constitutional safeguard of trial. We threaten him with a materially increased sanction if he avails himself of his right and is thereafter convicted. The sentencing differential is what makes plea bargaining coercive.

And in a footnote (p. 17) he raises the question whether the plea bargaining system is responsible for the high punishment level of the USA. He states:

> In the nineteenth and twentieth centuries, when the Europeans were ameliorating their sentences, we were not. It is tempting to wonder whether the requirements of the plea bargaining system have been somewhat responsible.

10.6 Depersonalization

A political decision to eliminate concern for the social background of the defendant involves much more than making these characteristics inappropriate for decisions on pain. By the same token, the offender is to a large extent excluded as a person. There is no point in exposing a social background, childhood, dreams, defeats – perhaps mixed with some glimmer from happy days – social life, all those small things which are essential to a perception of the other as a full human being. With the Sentencing Manual and its prime outcome, the Sentencing Table, crime is standardized as Offence Levels, a person's life as Criminal History Points, and decisions on the delivery of pain are reduced to finding the point where two lines merge. The right decision becomes a point in space, and pain.

The penal process thus acquires a similarity to what Georg Simmel (here 1950) describes from economic life. To him, money becomes the condensed, anti-individualistic unit that makes modern life possible. His concern is that modernity destroys autonomy and individuality.

> ... the individuality of phenomena is not commensurate with the pecuniary principle.
> ... These traits must also colour the contents of life and favour the exclusion of those irrational, instinctive, sovereign traits and impulses which aim at determining the mode of life from within, instead of receiving the general and precisely schematized form of life from without (pp.409-413).

For sentencing purposes, the defendant might as well not have been in court. Everything relates to the act, and to former acts defined as crimes. The offender has minimal opportunities to present her/himself as a usual and therefore peculiar member of the universe of humanity.

This decision-making system has the obvious consequence of creating distance from the person to be sentenced. When social attributes are eliminated, a seemingly "objective" and impersonal system is created. Harm is the monetary unit – harm with pain as its price. It is a system in full accord with normal bureaucratic standards, and at the same time extraordinarily well suited for power-holders.

Distance can be created physically by a long-range gun, socially by class, professionally by a trained incapacity to see the whole person as he would have been seen as neighbour, friend or lover. In an authority structure additional distance is created by acting according to orders. The Sentencing Table is such an order from above. The judge might be a soft one. He might sense a life in misery. But the Table is there. I am so sorry, but your offence-level is 38. This is not my personal decision, I just have to carry it out.

With this system of sentencing, the authorities will have considerably more control than before. A system for the registration of all decisions on sentencing has been developed, and more is to come (United States Sentencing Commission Annual Report 1989). This moves power one step up the ladder, one step away from possible identification with the offender, and one step closer to the central authorities.

Sentencing Commissions have now been established in several states in the USA: Minnesota, Oregon, Pennsylvania and Washington. Minnesota is generally seen as a highly successful case (e.g. von Hirsch 1982), while Tonry (1991, p. 309) calls the Federal one a disaster. But the basic principles behind their work seem to be the same. They create their simplistic tables based on types of crime and numbers of earlier convictions, and the answer is given.[2]

2 In a paper with the grim title "Penal Regressions", Radzinowicz (1991 a) has this to say:
I regard Sentencing Commissions as having total flaws of one kind or another. They should not be regarded as a solution to the problems which face contemporary sentencing policy ... To advise – yes, but not to direct (p. 434).

Chapter 11

Justice done, or managed?

Jokes in *The New Yorker* are sometimes incomprehensible to Europeans. We do not share the cultural background and do not always understand the symbols and their double meaning. Cultural symbols can only be understood in a context of shared experience.

To most people in our time, and on both sides of the Atlantic, the image of Lady Justice is familiar and packed with meaning. In one hand she holds scales, of course of an old fashioned type, based on the principle of balance. In the other she has a sword. Mostly she is blindfolded, and represented in white clothes.

This symbol is of great importance, but of course not to all people. Perhaps we can understand law better if we look at social systems where she is of no importance at all, and compare these with systems where she has a virtually sacred meaning. Let us do so by comparing three types of legal organization: Village Law, Representative Law, and Independent Law. This will be an ideal-typical description, an attempt to clarify some general principles behind legal arrangements.

11.1 Village law

... would be one where the symbol of Justice would have no meaning.

First, why should she be blindfolded in the village? Imagine a village with sufficient autonomy to decide on internal conflicts, with a long history – at least long enough to have established norms for what is right and what is wrong – and with relatively egalitarian relationships between people. In such a system, law would be a matter for all grown-ups living in the village. They would know the rules through participation. Even if legal decisions were to some extent formalized, the ownership of legal knowledge would not be monopolized. By living there, they would all know and would all be natural participants in the decision-making. These would not be simple decisions. Since there were no specialists, there would be no one with clear authority to delimit the volume or type of arguments. Discussions might last for days. Old histories would be renewed, earlier decisions brought forward.

In a very fundamental sense, such a village court would operate in close proximity to the villagers. Often all take part, all have relevant knowledge, and all have to live with the consequences of their decisions. But this description also makes it clear why Lady Justice is out of style in the village. Lady Justice is above everybody. She is in white, untouched and untouchable, not a part of the whole. And then blindfolded and with a sword in a situation where everything is relevant – where everything must be seen – and where a sword is impossible since that would mean conflicts which might destroy the village. Where authority is absent, consensus must be reached. The law of the village therefore tends towards civil solutions; compensations and compromises – not dichotomies of guilt/innocence and the delivery of pain to the loser.

These were the major features. But let me hasten to add: The law of the village would not necessarily be "just". In particular, it would give little protection to those without power and connections in the village. Females were often, but not always, in that position. It was a law for a time long since gone. But bits and pieces remain.

Reminiscences of the village tradition can be found in the term "justices of the peace". Where authority was neither strong nor distant, it was necessary to find solutions acceptable to the parties to create peace. The closer decision-makers are to the participants in a conflict, the more important this becomes. With peace, the peace-maker gets both honour and a better life for himself in peaceful surroundings.

Peace-makers therefore know the importance of finding common ground. But the peace-makers cannot be blindfolded. On the contrary, she or he will need every sense to get a feeling of what might be common ground, where the parties might meet in a compromise. And a sword would be an absolutely impossible piece of equipment, as it symbolizes the possible use of force.

11.2 Representative law

In the village, the image of Lady Justice is irrelevant. She cannot be understood. But children of modernity may also have difficulty with that image, particularly if they are strong defenders of local democracy. According to many values, it is a matter of course that it is a good thing that the institution of law is close to the people. This can take two forms:

that judges and prosecutors are democratically elected,
or
that legislators have a strong influence on what happens in courts.

An operationalization of the first form is to put Lady Justice up for direct election, to get her into a position as an elected judge. This sounds democratic, and even more so if the district attorney and the chief of police are also up for election. If they do not act according to the wishes of the electorate, they may be thrown out of office at the next election.

But why then, make Lady Justice blindfolded? It would be a self-contradiction to bring her close to the people, but blind to their arguments. The idea behind blindfolding justice is of course to make her objective, to prevent her from seeing and being influenced by what she is not supposed to see. But to be democratically elected means that Lady Justice can be dethroned if she does not decide as her electorate thinks. There is a built-in conflict here. A justice close to the people – even a justice ideally representing that people – is at the same time a justice under maximum control by that people. That is the village justice, where the image of Lady Justice had no place. But she is also out of place running in a modern election. To survive elections, she must both listen and see. Besides, in the realities of modern societies, to be democratically elected does not mean representing everybody. Down to 50 percent take part in elections. A victory means representing the majority of those casting their votes. Often this means representing 1/3, even down to 1/4 of the population, not the totality, and particularly not small enclaves which may differ from the majority in style and some basic values. Being close to the people therefore, in our types of society, means being close to only a segment of that population. At the same time it means being distant from situations where justice is left in peace to strike a balance between values of importance to the totality. This is particularly so in societies where strong influence is exerted by the mass media in combination with public opinion surveys. Mass media thrive on crime, and give a distorted picture of what it is all about. And the surveys reflect the resulting surface opinions, which in turn strengthen the tendencies in the media.

But Lady Justice is also an anachronism in the second form above, where what happens in court is controlled in minute detail by the legislature. Again, such control sounds fine, according to democratic ideals. All power to the people, therefore power to the legislature rather than to the judges.

And it is, of course, the task of the legislature to issue the laws, and has always been so in societies which see themselves as democracies. The real problem has to do with the level of specification of the laws issued by the legislature. A law may state:

theft is a crime which has to be punished,
or
theft is a crime which has to be punished by imprisonment for up to 3 years,
or
theft is a crime which has to be punished by imprisonment for from 2 to 3 years ,
or
theft of type 19 is a crime which has to be punished by imprisonment for 30 months.

The dean of Scandinavian penal law, Professor Johs. Andenæs, had this to say (1991, p. 386, my translation):

> Personally, I am critical of the change in relationship between the legislature and the courts which a detailed regulation of the courts' use of punishments represents ... In a political democracy, nothing can be said against the right of the legislators to make the basic choice of values, both as to what to criminalize and to the amount of punishment. But it is difficult at the level of legislature to create a concrete and realistic conception of the realities that the courts will meet in individual and concrete cases. It is a common experience that lay people react differently when they get to know the individual case than when they make general statements on crime and punishment. There is no reason to believe that this is not also true of parliamentarians.

Andenæs probably had his experience with lay judges in mind. It is often seen, and is confirmed in the literature, that these tend to be more lenient towards criminals than trained judges. They may argue in general for a crime policy of stern measures, but then they make an exception for the offender they meet in their particular case. There is such an abundance of special circumstances in this case; basically the defendant was a decent person, not a "real" criminal; at least she or he had suffered so much through life that a stern sanction would have been most unjust.

Sentencing Tables created by Sentencing Commissions represent the extreme case of Representative Law. Sentencing is completely controlled by the politicians, and the judge is to the same extent made impotent at the sentencing stage. The judge has no freedom to consider the peculiar character of any case. Courts can decide on the concrete facts; did the defendant do it or not? But the whole question of mitigating and aggravating factors is removed from their domain. In this situation, Lady Justice does not need to be blindfolded. She has nothing to look at, except a Table. Central authorities in the form of a Sentencing Commission have decided. And there is no need for her scales. The weighing, too, is done in the Table. The task has been simplified. No wonder things are speeding up, an advance for modernity. But her sword is easier to use than ever. A sword directed by a Table.

11.3 Independent law

Children come to some sort of agreement on rules. They learn them through making. Villagers in small scale systems inherit the basic principles of the legal system, but then – in a process of general participation – continue the game. Their discussion is one of norm clarification. Slowly, the whole complicated case is brought into the daylight. Arguments are sorted out, accepted or rejected, given weight, and added up. The process is more than a mere weighing in the scalepans of Justice. It is a process of repeatedly going into the facts, and then comparing facts with norms. What takes place is a sort of value-crystallization, a clarification to everybody of the basic values of the system.

Old-fashioned courts still have their roots in this tradition. A judge is not free as a child to decide the rules, nor as relatively free as a villager. This sort of judge is guided by law, and by training if he is a professional judge. But some room exists, some room for the unexpected, for those concerns no one had thought of before they were made obvious by being formulated.

But basically, this is undemocratic. Judges of this type are not close to the people, as in the village, or directed by the people, as in the case of representative law. Independent judge is the term we use. That independence may vary. The most extreme independence comes when judges get the job from a selection body of other judges, when they have their task for life, when the whole process of appeal remains in their hands, and when they are protected from the rest of society by wealth and/or rank.

It is easy to understand the democratic criticism of this type of judge. Detailed instructions from Parliament or Sentencing Commissions are one type of answer, one type of attempt to bring judges under control. Public opinion surveys are another. Such surveys can convey the views of the population which could be used as a standard for the right punishment. But the questions in polls do not go deep enough, and are in our time mostly pale reflections of stereotypes created by the media. Questionnaires are not answered under the burden of responsibility. Acts are the tests of opinions. Concrete acts. It is through ordinary people's responsible participation in concrete cases of decisions on the use of pain that we get insights into their principles of justice. It is only when they personally have to decide on the use of pain, and preferably have to carry out the decision themselves, that we get to know the basic views emerging from the process of participation.

Perhaps we must accept that there is no way out. Maybe the old idea of some distance between the executive, legislative, and judicial powers has something to be said for it. And in this situation, the idea of Lady Justice acquires a meaning. The old-fashioned judge is a free person, but there are limits. Some fundamental values are supposed to be at the bottom of her or his reasoning. The decisions are not for sale. This is where the blindfolding of Lady Justice comes in. She must not be influenced by irrelevancies – money, connections, kinship. She has to stay clean – white, and she needs her scales. Her task is complicated. The central question in legal struggles has always had to do with what it is permissible to put onto her scales. First, what sort of arguments it is permissible to put on, and thereafter what weight those arguments can be given.

11.4 The silent revolution

No wonder modern managers often leave old-fashioned court rooms in disgust. They may be there as witnesses, as victims, or charged with a crime. And they meet the formalities: gowns, probably everybody rising when the judge enters, perhaps oaths with a hand on the Bible. Then the slow pace, the detailed documentation, the endless repetitions until it is all over – or so the manager thinks until he learns that it takes weeks, or even months before the verdict arrives.

It is easy to understand the manager's impatience. Compared to decision-making machineries of the type he knows from modern industry, the courts stand out as archaic. They are out of place in modern times, and must be changed.

Which is exactly what happens.

The American system of justice has been undergoing revolutionary development these last few years. But the country seems not to be quite aware of its own revolution. No wonder. The first industrial revolution arrived with noisy and smoky machinery, of which no one could remain unaware. The characteristic feature of modern production on the other hand, and of the present revolutionary process, is its silence. Most of it takes place at the symbolic level. Money is moved around by means of small signs conveyed electronically. To a large extent, the product is symbols, words, perspectives, new ways of conceiving life and organizing life. The recent revolution is gentle in appearance, peaceful, and promises comfort to many people.

On the legal side, the law and order system is quietly, but highly efficiently, adapting to modernity, adapting to becoming a child of industrialization. Central values here are the clarification of goals, production control, cost reduction, rationality, and the division of labour, all combined with the coordination of all actions at a higher level of command. We are back both to Max Weber and to a system of extreme efficiency in reaching those clearly defined goals.

As formulated in further written comments on this book from Flemming Balvig:

> The adaptation can be seen in the physical changes taking place within the court-rooms. Slowly, these rooms take the form of an office of a junior director in a large firm. Gone are the gowns. The old paintings on the wall are exchanged for modern lithographs, forms of expressions become more straight forward, the seating arrangements more similar to those for ordinary decision-makers. The computer gets a natural place in the room. The radiation of solemn power, old heritage and justice is exchanged for comfort and efficiency.

The adaptation can also be seen in the output of the penal system. Production is faster, many more people can be sentenced with much less effort than before. Decisions are more uniform. Similar acts seen as crimes are punished more equally. For those who define justice as equality, and equality as accomplished when all persons with the same criminal record and committing the same act are met with exactly the same type of intended pain, the level of justice has risen. Predictability within the system has also increased. Any child can read the Sentencing Table, find the Offence level of contemplated acts, and decide if it is worth it.

The major bottlenecks have been removed. Plea bargaining ensures fast confessions, and the sentencing manuals ensure fast decisions on punishment. This creates almost unlimited scope for processing cases. The manuals are bound to be computerised soon, if this has not already been done. With all the relevant factors built in, a secretary can prepare everything up to the point when the judge touches the final button giving the intervals of choice – and soon, no doubt, also the preferred alternative within the intervals.

Speed, accountability, similarity, clear messages to potential criminals, a system which offers easily operated control by central authorities in the form of a Sentencing Commission, which again is under the control of the elected representatives of the people, amounts to a perfect adaptation to modernity.

And once more: What happens in the USA also takes place elsewhere. Even England and Wales are on their way towards more central control of the judiciary. In a White Paper on Crime, Justice and Protecting the Public (Home Office 1990), the just deserts model is hailed. It comes as point I in the Summary of the main proposals from the Government:

> – a coherent legislative framework for sentencing, with the severity of the punishment matching the seriousness of the crime ...

And then on pp. 1–2:

> The Court of Appeal has issued guidance, which the Government very much welcomes, for sentencing some of the more serious offences tried in the Crown Court. The Magistrates' Association has prepared provisional guidelines for cases tried in magistrates' courts. However, there is still too much uncertainty and little guidance about the principles which should govern sentencing. There is a similar uncertainty about the release of prisoners on parole.
> ...
> The Government is therefore proposing a new and more coherent statutory framework for sentencing. It will build on the guidance already given by the Court of Appeal.
> ...
> The aim of the Government's proposals is better justice through a more consistent approach to sentencing, so that convicted criminals get their

"just deserts". The severity of the sentence of the court should be directly related to the seriousness of the offence.

But there are still limits to governmental interference in England and Wales (pp. 8–9):

> The legislation will be in general terms. It is not the Government's intention that Parliament should bind the courts with strict legislative guidelines. The courts have shown great skill in the way they sentence exceptional cases. The courts will properly continue to have the wide discretion they need if they are to deal justly with the great variety of crimes which comes before them. The Government rejects a rigid statutory framework, on the lines of those introduced in the United States, or a system of minimum or mandatory sentences for certain offences. This would make it more difficult to sentence justly in exceptional cases. It would also result in more acquittals by juries, with more guilty men and women going free unjustly as a result.

So, two steps forward, and one back in England and Wales. But the position of an Attorney General is a new one in these countries. Through systematic appeals, that office will probably result in decreased variance in sentencing, and – it seems from the White Paper – represent a pressure in the direction of materializing ideas of just deserts. The Government also promises to make arrangements for training sentencers to give effect to the new sentencing policies and the more detailed interpretation of the legislation by the Court of Appeal. Furthermore:

> The new legislative provisions, the maximum penalties for each offence, the guidance from the Court of Appeal and the Attorney General's new power to refer over-lenient sentences for very serious offenders to the Court of Appeal, should all contribute to the development of coherent sentencing practice, which can be disseminated to the courts by the Judicial Studies Board. Against *this* (italics mine) background, the Government sees no need for a Sentencing Council to develop sentencing policies or guidance.

Maybe the step back was only a half one.

11.5 Expressive behaviour

Modernity is rationality. But some aspects of crime go beyond rationality. For the victim, the case – if it is a serious one – is most often a one-time occurrence. It is a highly loaded emotional affair. If the crime is perceived as a serious one, the victim may have feelings of anger, or even grief. No courts – except of the village type – are particularly good at coping with such emotions. Most are dull and task-oriented. The victim is not a major character in the play; the case is directed by people claiming to represent the parties. This distance from the victim may be one reason for victim dissatisfaction and the many statements that criminals get away with their misdeeds too easily. Demands for stiffer penalties may be a result of lack of attention to the needs of victims for expressive outlets, rather than of wishes for vengeance.

One way of correcting this would be to give the victim a more central position in the proceedings, while also attempting to reduce the utility-oriented character of the whole operation. I have in other connections tried to compare anger and grief (Christie 1987). Death is an occurrence which often results in extreme grief. At funerals it is legitimate to express some of it. To my knowledge, nobody has – as yet – dared to tamper with this situation. There is no health-propaganda on the walls of the Crematorium: "If he had not smoked, we would not have been here today." Funerals may be one of the few remaining arenas for expressive behaviour.

Courts have for a long time been badly suited as expressive arenas. With modernity they move from bad to worse. Detailed instructions for sentencing, particularly computerized ones, may be as foreign to the sentencing process as they would be in the interaction between a sinner and a priest. Vengeance regulated by a table or by pressing a button represents one step further away from a situation where anger and grief are given legitimate outlets. The system has moved from expressive ritualism to managerial efficiency.

Some of the explosion in the US figures may relate to a sort of inter-institutional misunderstanding. The institution of the law has come too close to politics, at the same time as utility-thinking borrowed from the institution for production seems to have been given what appears to be absolute dominance.

Chapter 12

Modernity and behaviour control

12.1 Children of modernity

The title of this chapter was selected with care. Its intention is to establish a link to Zygmunt Bauman's important book on *Modernity and the Holocaust* (1989).

Bauman represents the third wave in understanding the extermination camps during the Second World War.

First came the wave of explaining the camps as the product of abnormal minds. From Hitler all the way down to the guards in the camps, those who worked there were seen as deviants, mad, and of course bad, or as disturbed authoritarian personalities (Adorno et al. *1950),* or at least as under the command of others of that sort. How else could the horror be explained, how else could it be understood that the country of Goethe and Schiller and the most advanced of sciences went so wrong?

The second wave of explanations moved from deviant persons to deviant social systems. The atrocities had something to do with deep defects in the German nation, perhaps with peculiar political constellations, all triggered by persons of the type described in wave one, the bad or mad or deeply authoritarian people. Normal people commit abnormal acts when situations become abnormal. I have myself written in that tradition on guards in concentration camps (Christie 1952–53).

The third wave is radically different. Here, extermination is not seen as an exception, but as a logical extension of our major type of social organization. In this perspective, the Holocaust becomes a natural outgrowth of our type of society, not an exception to it. Extermination becomes a child of modernity, not a return to an earlier stage of barbarism. The conditions for the Holocaust are precisely those that have helped to create the industrial society: the division of labour, the modern bureaucracy, the rational spirit, the efficiency, the scientific mentality, and particularly the relegation of values from important sectors of society. From this perspective, the Holocaust is one example, but only one, of what might happen where large sectors of activities are exempted from being evaluated by the total set of values – the ordinary home-standards of decency. The commander of Auschwitz would probably not have invited his favourite aunt for a visit. One of the doctors invited his wife – to his great regret (Lifton 1986).

Extermination camps were like blueprints of rationally organized societies. As expressed by Bauman (pp. 11–12):

> ... none of the societal conditions that made Auschwitz possible has truly disappeared, and no effective measures have been undertaken to prevent such possibilities and principles from generating Auschwitzlike catastrophes.
> ...
> I propose that the experience of the Holocaust, now thoroughly researched by the historians, should be looked upon as, so to speak, a sociological "laboratory". The Holocaust has exposed and examined such attributes of our society as are not revealed, and hence are not empirically accessible, in "non-laboratory" conditions. In other words, *I propose to treat the Holocaust as a rare, yet significant and reliable, test of the hidden possibilities of modern society.*

The happy optimists,[1] all the believers in steady and endless progress for humanity, are not given much comfort in Bauman's book. There

---

1 Norbert Elias (1978, 1982) is often seen as one of these. His optimistic perspective is this: From living under conditions demanding a constant readiness to fight, and with free play of the emotions in defence of one's life and possessions from physical attack, we have moved into a complex society demanding civility and personal restraint. But in extreme contrast to his message stands its dedication: To the memory of his parents, dead in Breslau 1940 and Auschwitz 1941. The behaviour of – or for – states seems to a large extent to be outside of the interests of Elias in these books. For a more positive view on Elias, see Garland (1986).

exists a hidden alliance of believers in progress, and even more believe in the modern "gardening state" who view society as an object for designing, cultivating and weed-poisoning. Bauman is in strong opposition to all this. He works in the tradition of Ivan Illich and the group around him – most recently manifested in the "Dictionary of Progress" (Sachs 1992). To Bauman, the Holocaust is more than its own horrors. It is also a warning sign. Up to now it is the clearest indicator that industrialization does not mean progress, that we are on the wrong track, and that the cure cannot be just getting more of the same.

Bauman warns against the Jewish tendency to monopolize Holocaust, to make it into a phenomenon peculiar to the Jews. Ivan Illich is on the same line and argues (oral comunication) that the attention given to anti-Semitism has made us blind to the more general roots of extermination. This monopolization also makes us blind to the destiny of all the other groups – gypsies, homosexuals, communists in the concentration camps – and of the supposed opponents of the Soviet-regime in the Gulags.

The central part of Bauman's explanation of Holocaust is the *social production of moral indifference in modern societies.* That indifference was created by authorization, by routinization and by dehumanization of the victims by ideological definitions and indoctrinations.

Bureaucratization was essential in this process. As stated by Hilberg in his monumental study of *The Destruction of the European Jews* (1985, vol. III, p. 1011):

> A Western bureaucracy had never before faced such a chasm between moral precepts and administrative action; an administrative machine had never been burdened with such a drastic task. In a sense the task of destroying the Jews put the German bureaucracy to a supreme test.

And they were not peculiar people. From top to bottom, they were just ordinary. Hilberg continues his point:

> Any member of the Order Police could be a guard at a ghetto or on a train. Every lawyer in the Reichs Security Main Office was presumed to be suitable for leadership in the mobile killing units; every finance expert to the Economic-Administrative Main Office was considered a natural choice for

service in a death camp. In other words, all necessary operations were accomplished with whatever personnel were at hand.

Extermination was not decided on from the outset. At first, the goal was to make Germany judenfrei – free of Jews. But then Austria was added, and also had to be free of Jews. They could be dumped in the eastern territories, but local administrators protested. Madagascar was seen as a possibility; Eichmann spent a whole year on that idea, but Britain ruled the waves, and Eichmann was ordered to change his plans into physical extermination:

> The rest was the matter of co-operation between various departments of state bureaucracy; of careful planning, designing proper technology and technical equipment, budgeting, calculating and mobilizing necessary resources. ... the choice was an effect of the earnest effort to find rational solutions to successive "problems" as they arose in the changing circumstances. (Bauman pp. 16–17).

The process was not directed by monsters. It was organized by the Section of Administration and Economy. It was run with precision and speed, and according to calculable universalistic rules. "Irrationality" was excluded throughout. People suspected of enjoying killing would most definitely be excluded.

Being so rational, the process was in harmony with basic elements of the civilizing process, a process characterized by the relentless elimination of violence from social life. Or, in an important addition by Bauman, a process characterized by the concentration of violence under state control. What takes place here also requires the silencing of morality as a major concern. Bauman says (the italics are his) (pp. 28–29):

> ... *the civilizing process is, among other things, a process of divesting the use and deployment of violence from moral calculus, and of emancipating the desiderata of rationality from interference of ethical norms or moral inhibitions.*

> ... the conditions of the rational conduct of business – like the notorious separation between the household and the enterprise, or between private income and the public purse – function at the same time as powerful factors in isolating the end-orientated, rational action from interchange with

processes ruled by other (by definition, irrational) norms, and thus rendering it immune to the constraining impact of the postulates of mutual assistance, solidarity, reciprocal respect etc., which are sustained in the practice of non-business formations.

To Bauman, the Holocaust was not an irrational outflow of barbarian tendencies, but a legitimate resident in the house of modernity. And I want to add: Holocaust is only a continuation of a major trend of European colonial history.

We are just now into a stream of Centennial years for several of the great European victories in Africa. The intellectual foundation for what turned into unbelievable atrocities was the theories of development and the survival of the fittest. The tools for the survival of the fittest were guns against arrows. Did Hitler learn his methods from Stalin? is the theme of the debate among historians and sociologists in Germany. Nonsense, says Lindqvist (1992, pp. 199–200). Hitler knew it from childhood. The air surrounding him, and also all other Europeans at the time of his youth, was saturated by the conviction that imperialism was a biological necessity leading to the inevitable extermination of the lower races. The nine-year-old Adolf Hitler was not in the Albert Hall on May 4 1898. It was on this great occasion – at the peak of victories in Africa – that Lord Salisbury, the Prime Minister of Great Britain, stated that the nations of the world can be divided into the dying and those alive. Hitler was not there. Even so he knew, as all Europeans knew. They knew what France had done in Africa, what England had done, and, as late-comers, what Germany had done as close to our time as 1904. Dying nations were in need of some help to get it over with.

Thus, extermination is nothing new. We should not be that shocked. Hitler's and Stalin's camps were just parts of an old tradition. But it took place inside Europe. That meant they came closer – and at the same time became more incomprehensible.

12.2 Cloth of the devil

Thoughts are unthinkable only until formulated. Here it comes:

Hitler's idea was one of Volk, of purity of the stock, and of space – Lebensraum – for the purified product. He had the capacity to realise it. The extermination camp was a product of industrialization, one product among others of a combination of thought-patterns, social organization and technical tools. My contention is that the prison system in the USA is rapidly moving in the same direction. It is also highly likely that this trend will spread into other industrialized countries, particularly in Eastern Europe. It will be more surprising if this does not take place, than if it takes place in this decade.

To some, the very idea that criminal policy in industrial democratic societies could bear the slightest resemblance to Nazi times and extermination camps sounds absurd. Most of our highly industrialised societies are democratically run, and have protection against crime as their goal, not extermination.

This is of course true. And I do not think prisons in modern industrial societies will end up as direct carbon copies of the camps. Even if the worst comes to the worst, most prisoners will not intentionally be killed in modern prison systems. A number of death sentences will be effectuated, but most prisoners will eventually be released or die by suicide, by violence during incarceration,[2] or from natural causes. Gulags are, therefore, a more relevant term for what might come than concentration camps. My gloomy suggestion is limited to saying that a large proportion of males from the lower classes may end up living their most active lives in prisons or camps. I am not even saying that this will certainly happen, but the chances are not small. Industrial progress and civilization have no built-in guarantees against such a development.

On the contrary, we can see energetic first beginnings, in the changes in the legal apparatus, in the ideology of just deserts, in the growth and efficiency of the controlling forces, in the increased numbers of prisoners, and also in the rationale for handling these prisoners. Malcolm Feeley (1991b, pp. 66-67) talks about "the new penology". By this he

2 Human Rights Watch (1992) reports (p. 38) that assassination by fellow inmates has been the second or third leading cause of death in state prisons over the past ten years or so, with the first cause being illnesses and other natural causes, and suicides and inmate-to-inmate homicides alternating in second place.

means a penology which is not oriented towards individuals, and particularly not towards changing these individuals through rehabilitation or punishment, but instead focuses on management of aggregate populations.

> The task is managerial not transformative.
>
> ...
>
> The tools for this enterprise are "indicators", prediction tables, classification schemes in which individualized diagnosis and response is displaced by aggregate classification systems for purposes of surveillance, confinement, and control.
>
> A central feature of the new penalty is the replacement of moral or clinical description of the individual with an actuarial language of probabilistic calculations and statistical distributions applied to populations.

To Feeley, this new penal policy is neither about punishing, nor about rehabilitating individuals at fault. It is instead about identifying and managing unruly groups. From our perspective in this book, just what is needed in the control of the dangerous classes. And greatly helped in performing the task by the distance created through the new penology; from individuals to categories, from morality to management and actuarial thinking.

If we want to control the Devil, we must know him. We must understand the general principles behind what happened in Germany – and preferably also in the USSR – and then try to translate those principles into whatever is relevant to an understanding of our own situation here and now.

But the Devil has his tricks. He changes his costumes. If we want to unmask the Devil, we have to see him as a general category, and on that basis understand how he will appear next time.

A first step towards such an understanding is to look out for major strains and tensions in our present structure and ask: How do these more important problems in our industrialized nations manifest themselves?

Hitler purified the stock and saw a need for Lebensraum. The superindustrialized states have the two problems we have already pointed out: first, to find Lebensraum for their products; second, to find a solution for those no longer needed when the efficiency of the machinery increases.

And here comes the unpleasant observation: We have seen that prisons are most helpful with both problems. In the most stable of welfare states, strict penal action against the most provocative non-contributors gives room for a policy of welfare for the remainder. In other industrialized nations, imprisonment means control of the dangerous classes. But in addition, and of increasing importance, comes the fact that the whole institution of crime control in itself is a part of the system of production. The system is of great economic interest to both owners and workers. It is a system of production of vital importance to modern societies. It produces control. In this perspective, the problem arises: when is enough, enough? There is a built-in drive for expansion in industrialization. What will happen to criminal policy if the industrial development continues?

12.3 Limits to growth?

There are no "natural limits" in this area. There are no limits on raw materials, or green movements creating trouble for the industry. We are all sinners before God, and most of us have committed acts for which we could have been brought before state authorities, had there been sufficient interest in penalising us. However that may be, it is quite clear that a much greater part of the population than the present catch could be drawn into the net, if it were made sufficiently strong and fine-meshed to hold them.

Sufficient reason for stopping the expansion of the prison system could be found if industrial development as a whole came to a halt. That would shatter the dream of free enterprise. Many who had never been near the poverty line would experience that unemployment was not necessarily a result of lack of initiative, idleness, or a hedonistic life-style. The flow of money for the control industry would also dry up. Taxpayers' money – from the few who would have anything to pay – would have to be reserved for even more essential needs.

However, a deep recession is also a situation in which prisons may be seen as the most essential of all needs. In a deep recession, the dangerous class increases in size, and becomes more dangerous than ever before. As we have seen, the lower classes are already massively over-represented in all prison systems we know of.

There are no natural limits. The industry is there. The capacity is there. Two-thirds of the population will have a standard of living vastly above any found – for so large a proportion of a nation – anywhere else in the world. Mass media flourish on reports on the dangers of the crimes committed by the remaining one-third of the population. Rulers are elected on promises to keep the dangerous third behind bars. Why should this come to a stop? There are no natural limits for rational minds.

The driving forces are so overwhelmingly strong. The interests behind them are in harmony with basic values. They are morally so solidly founded. Why should they not, in the foreseeable future, succeed completely?

Germany was able to do it, to reach a final solution in the middle of a war, despite the urgent need to make alternative use of its railways as well as of the guards. The USSR was able to develop the Gulags in the midst of preparations for war, and to run them during and after it. They were not only able to do so, but benefited from the arrangements. Why should not modern, industrialized nations be even more successful?

Hitler and his people were facing a close to impossible task. So were the leaders of the USSR. How much easier will it not be to manage the new dangerous classes?

The ground has been prepared. The media prepare it every day and night. Politicians join ranks with the media. It is impossible politically not to be against sin. This is a competition won by the highest bidder. To protect people from crime is a cause more just than any. At the same time, the producers of control are eagerly pushing for orders. They have the capacity. There are no natural limits. A crime-free society is such a sacred goal for so many, that even money does not count. Who asks about costs in the middle of a total war? Management stems from the word ménage. The master model manager is the man with the whip, driving his horses around the ring. The success of management is related to its ability to simplify value structures. This condition seems to be fulfilled in modern society.

12.4 Industrialized killing

German industry was most helpful in realizing the "final solution". For extermination a gas was used called Zyklon. The gas had to be bought from private firms. According to Hilberg (1985, p. 886), the enterprises that furnished it were part of the chemical industry, specializing in disinfecting buildings, barracks and clothes in specially constructed gas chambers. The company that developed the gas method was the Deutsche Gesellschaft für Schädlingsbekämpfung – DEGESCH. The firm was owned by three corporations: I.G. Farben (42.5 per cent), Deutsche Gold- und Silber-Scheideanstalt (42.5 per cent) and Goldsmidt (15 per cent). The profit in 1942 was 760,000 Reichsmark.[3] Business went on as usual until late in the war. One plant was bombed and heavily damaged in March 1944. At this time, the SS was making preparations to send 750,000 Jews to Auschwitz, then the only killing centre still in existence. But TESTA made it once more. 2,800 kgs of Zyklon were shipped to Auschwitz. According to Hilberg (p. 891), the firm – "hurriedly inquired who was to be billed". The supply was kept up to the very end.

I.G. Farben participated in producing the gas for Auschwitz. But it was not certain they knew what they were doing. The sales of Zyklon B doubled from 1938 to 1943. But the gas was also used for other purposes, particularly delousing military equipment like barracks and submarines. One ton of Zyklon was sufficient for killing one million people. In 1943, 411 tons were produced (Hayes 1987, p. 362).

3 "The Zyklon was produced by two companies: the Dessauer Werke and the Kaliwerke at Kolin. An I.G. Farben plant (at Uerdingen) produced the stabilizer for the Zyklon. Distribution of the gas was controlled by DEGESCH, which in 1929 divided the world market with an American corporation, Cyanamid. However, DEGESCH did not sell Zyklon directly to users. Two other firms handled the retailing: HELI and TESTA. The territory of these two corporations was divided by a line ... (this) gave to HELI mostly private customers and to TESTA mainly the governmental sector, including the Wehrmacht and the SS."

Therefore, the producers might have been unaware of the use of their products in the extermination of humans. None of the leaders of I.G. Farben was later made responsible for this aspect of the atrocities.

But they had to breathe while visiting their factories. One site was next to Auschwitz. The camp provided the slave-workers for the construction work. Even the top-executives could not escape the "pervasive stench emanating from the crematoria of Auschwitz and Birkenau". The stench – "simply overwhelmed the official explanation that the camps' continuous battle with typhus forced the burning of dead bodies". (Hayes 1987, p. 364). Moreover, the slave-workers were well aware of the destiny prepared for them. Supervisors from I.G. Farben "not only spoke openly of the gassing, but wielded it as an incentive to work harder". In some mines close by, also run by I.G. Farben, the conditions were even worse. Food was better, but the life expectancy in these mines dropped to somewhere between four and six weeks.

Five leaders of I.G. Farben were sentenced after the war for their use of slave-labour. The punishments were light, and some of the reasons given by the court are of relevance to the discussion on private prisons:

> we cannot say that a private citizen shall be placed in a position of being compelled to determine in the heat of war whether his government is right or wrong, or, if it starts right, when it turns wrong (Quoted in Hayes, 1985, p. 332).

In 1951, the last of the leaders of I.G. Farben were out of prison. Thereafter, they all returned to prominence and prosperity as advisers or officers in numerous German corporations. And why not, asks Hayes (1987 p. 380 and 382):

> Farben's leaders chose to behave in this situation like businessmen, not revolutionaries.
>
> ...
>
> Their sense of professional duty encouraged them to regard every issue principally in terms of their special competences and responsibilities, in this case, to their fields and stockholders. In obeying this mandate, they relieved themselves of the obligation to make moral or social judgements or to examine the overall consequences of their decisions.

12.5 Medicalized killing

It cannot happen here. We live in democracies. We know more. Our populations have much higher levels of general education. Most importantly, we have moved into societies which are greatly influenced by the highest professional standards.

Yet those of us who have worked with problems concerning the concentration camps remain unimpressed or, worse still, filled with the deepest distrust.

What happened back in the days of extermination was precisely that the professionals did the job, in beautiful cooperation with the bureaucracy.

Scientists were essential participants. The most basic idea was purification of the stock. The not-so-pure ought not to produce children, the pure ought to produce many. Sterilisation of the unwanted and a productivity bonus to the pure followed. Those were not deviant thoughts. US scientists reported home, with envy, how ideas of race hygiene, ideas also valid in the USA, were actually being tried out in Germany.

But some unwanted people continued to appear, like the physically handicapped. They were seen as having "lives not worth living", and in a secret decree euthanasia was authorised. As the war approaches, the criteria for those to be killed widened from physical defects into mental ones. First, this was limited to the seriously mentally handicapped, then the not so seriously retarded were included, then the insane, then the psychopaths, the homosexuals, and, as cases beyond discussion in all these categories, anybody with the wrong racial background. Perfect tools were developed. Ordinary shooting proved expensive and caused the killers mental strain. Injections were less efficient than poisonous fumes from car engines. But insecticides in the form of gas proved best of all, and were accordingly used.

Doctors were essential. Medical analogies were used all the time. The German nation was seen as a body. That whole body had to be treated. When a part is sick, surgery is needed. Jews were cancer – the need to cut off the infected part of the social body was obvious. It was not killing, it was treatment. Doctors translated theory into action, and reported back to the theoreticians. They were in positions to act in person, simply by virtue of being doctors. Medicalized killing is what Lifton (1986) calls it. He interviewed twenty-nine men who had been significantly involved at high levels with Nazi medicine. Five had worked in concentration camps. He also interviewed former Nazi non-medical professionals of some prominence. And lastly, he interviewed eighty former Auschwitz prisoners who had worked on medical blocks. More than half of them were doctors. A major finding in this study is the importance of medical thinking both in preparing the whole operation, and also in the concrete actions of extermination. Even on the railway-platforms, where the trains from the ghettos arrived, doctors were always present. There, on the spot, they decided on the concrete cases of surgery on the national body; a nod to the left – immediate extermination, a nod to the right – a sort of life in the camp for forced labour. If there were no doctors available, a dentist would do, or a pharmacist. It was important not to give ground on this point: it had to be a medical decision. Without doctors, or those close to them, on the platform, it would have been killing.

The worst nightmare will never materialize. The dangerous population will not be exterminated, except for those killed by capital punishment. But the risks are great that those seen as core members of the dangerous population may be confined, warehoused, stored away, and forced to live their most active years as consumers of control. It can be done democratically, and under the strict control of the legal institutions.

12.6 Legalized killing

– if the Holocaust was a child of industrialized society,
– if rational bureaucratic methods were a major condition for getting it all done,
– if scientific theories played an important part,
– if medical thinking was another essential condition for doing the unthinkable,

– then, there is every reason to expect similar phenomena to reappear, if the time is ripe and the essential conditions are there.

Are they?

The industrialized societies are there, more than ever, and are also under more strain than ever. Market economy rules the world, with an "obvious" demand for rationality, utility, and, of course, profit. The lower classes, easily transformed into the dangerous classes, are there. So are scientific theories with potential for action. Drug theories are there to the effect that certain drugs – not those already in heavy use, but some new ones – are supposed to be of such a nature that the most severe of methods of investigation and penalties are legitimate in the fight against them. And the theoreticians in criminology and law are there with a helping hand. Nobody believes in treatment any more, but incapacitation has been a favourite since the birth of the positivistic theories of crime control.[4]

And the system of law adapts itself most beautifully to the demands of modern times. The idea of just deserts makes it possible to streamline the system, and particularly to disregard all other values than the

---

4 The International Association of Criminal Policy (Internalionale Kriminalistische Vereinigung) was founded in 1889. The central figure was von Liszt, insisting on helping nature to control the dangerous classes, particularly the 'incorrigible', those basic opponents of social order. Again and again, von Liszt insisted that those who could not be reformed were to be incapacitated. According to Radzinowicz (1991b) he regarded the control of this group as the central and most urgent task of criminal policy:

About seventy per cent of all prisoners were recidivists and at least half of them should be designated as 'incorrigible habitual offenders'. Against them society must protect itself and, "as we do not wish to behead or to hang and cannot transport", what is left is detention for life or for an indeterminate period (p. 39).

... every offender convicted for the third time should be regarded as an incorrigible offender and as such should be committed to this type of quasi permanent segregation (p. 40).

The Habitual Offender had to be made harmless at *his expense* (von Liszt's italics) 'not ours', writes Radzinowicz (p. 40), and makes von Liszt sound highly modern.

Naucke (1982, p. 557) has this to say about the Marburger Program formulated by von Liszt:

This theory is at the disposal of those who control the penal law. The Marburger program contains no instrument to differentiate between those who ought to be offered this service, and those who ought to be denied it.

question of the gravity of the act. The ideal of matching the gravity of a crime with a portion of pain has the consequence that all other basic values that courts traditionally have to weigh are forced out of the proceedings. What was a system of justice is converted into a system of crime control. The classical distinction between the judiciary, the executive and the legislature has to a large extent dissolved. The courts become tools in the hands of politicians or, in the most extreme cases, the judges – as well as the prosecutors – become politicians themselves. Yet this is above criticism. It has none of the grave illegalities about it that marked the Holocaust or the Gulags. Now it is democratic crime control by the voting majority. To this there are no natural limits, as long as the actions do not hurt that majority.

There are no particular reasons for optimism. There is no easy way out, no prescription for a future where the worst will not come to the worst. Working with words, I have nothing more than words to offer: Words, attempts to clarify the situation we are in, attempts to make visible some of the values being pushed aside in recent hectic attempts to adapt to demands that are in fashion just now. Let us look once more into the institution of justice to see if there may not after all be something of value in some of the old forms of that institution.

Chapter 13

Crime control as culture

13.1 The common core

Taiwan accepts Organs This was the headline over a little Note in *Corrections Digest,* November 27, 1991. And then follows:

> Thirty-seven organs of 14 executed Taiwan criminals have been donated for transplants, a Japanese transplant specialist on Sept. 30 quoted a Taiwan surgeon as saying. Masami Kizaki, chairman of the Japan Society for Transplantation, said Chun-Jan-Lee, a professor at National Taiwan University, revealed the transplants. Dr. Lee said the condemned criminals agreed to give their hearts, kidneys and livers "to be redeemed from sin". The donors were shot dead while on respirators so their blood circulation and breathing would not stop suddenly.

Again a sort of disbelief in my own eyes. It can't be done. It just can't be! But obviously it can. It was done.

And I look around, wondering, who will take action, who will go to the barricades in protest?

The *doctors?*

Why should they protest? Some would, but not necessarily because they were doctors.

Those killed were satisfied, at least with this particular aspect. The recipients of the organs were happy. The doctors might also be happy

– so much health for what otherwise would only have been waste and misery. At least this would be better than cheating Turkish labourers out of their kidneys, as in England, or buying them from people in need, as in India. Some lay people may have difficulty in understanding and accepting it, but doctors are trained in rational reasoning. It is almost a miracle. A blind person may get his sight back, the husband and father with a failing heart would after transplantation live a long life with his wife and children.

Some would still not be convinced, and think that the *judges* would protest. People trained in law would not allow capital punishment to be used in this way?

That would depend on the law. There may have been no laws against it, or even more dramatically, there may have been laws encouraging the practice. If shooting sentenced people while they were in respirators was the law of the country, the judges would accept it, regardless of vague feelings of uneasiness, regardless of lay reactions, regardless of surprised questions from wives and children at home after strenuous days in courts.

Hitler had the same problem.

Ordinary people had difficulty in understanding and accepting his program for the improvement of the German nation. Serious problems appeared in the early stages of the operation. The first known and officially authorized killing of an extremely handicapped child was initiated and accepted by a father. Even then, it was kept secret. But as the program was enlarged, and the criteria for "life not worth living" were widened, there were unpleasant outbursts of protest in the German population. Relatives asked for details on why and where those close to them had died. There were also unpleasant episodes of protests from local residents close to the sites of extermination and cremation. Religious groups joined forces. This brought the program to a halt – inside Germany. But now the machinery was ready, and when the war broke out most of it was moved from Germany and into the occupied territories, enlarged, and used in the way we know so well.

What am I trying to say?

I am trying to say that Charles H. Cooley (1909,1956) is right. Cooley, that great and by now generally forgotten father of sociology in the USA, had the idea that all humans had a common ground. All humans were basically similar, not because of biology, but because they shared a basic human experience. They shared the experience of being the most vulnerable of all beings during a longer period after birth than any other beings, and of being doomed to an early death if not cared for. We all, basically, have this shared human experience. If not, we are not humans. How could it otherwise be, asks Cooley, that we can read the Greek dramas, find them relevant and important to our present lives, and understand what they are all about? As I read Cooley, he finds in this shared experience the basis of a common core in humanity, a basis of shared values and rules on how to act. We all have some common gut-feelings of right and wrong, and some common basis for sensing when impossible conflicts arise. We are all, lay as well as learned, trained in law from age zero, and have built into our minds large and often conflict-filled data-bases on moral questions for our remaining lives. A Norwegian term for this knowledge would be "folkevett" or, to use a slightly more old-fashioned term, "den folkelige fornuft", a sort of intuitive common sense shared by everyone.

This view is basically an optimistic one. Those who survive childhood have been helped to do so. They have experienced at least a minimum, and in many cases a maximum, of social contact and care and warmth, and have thereby also absorbed the basic rules of social life. If not, they would not have grown up. The problems are the same, everywhere. So are the stored experiences.

This common core is surprisingly resistant. Humans have experience of being social beings. It is not without reason that Durkheim (1966) has altruistic suicide as one of his major types. Humans go into death for each other. That is normal, if they are ordinary people, if altruism is necessary, and if the parties are close enough to perceive each other as human beings. But this last point on closeness is important and relevant to us all. Most of us also have limits to our obligations. That is necessary for survival. We are all trapped in the old ethical dilemma: how can I eat when I know that people, right now, less than 6 hours' flight away, are starving to death? I eat, and survive.

So did, for a while, the Jewish police in the ghetto of Lodz. This ghetto was the largest in the Eastern occupied territories. Lodz was an old, highly industrialized city, a sort of Manchester of Poland. M.G, Rumkowski, the Eldest of the Jews and with absolute power inside the ghetto, had the idea that they could survive by making themselves indispensable to the German war machine. The ghetto became as one large factory, extremely well organized, with high discipline and no trouble with organized labour. Some young workers tried, but were easily pacified. But the SS officers were never completely satisfied. Inside the barbed wire fence, the ghetto had largely independent self-government. But the Germans inspected. They saw very old people around, and small children, non-productive consumers, and ordered them out of the ghetto to a "more comfortable place" in the country-side. Some accepted, until car-loads of used clothes came back and the realities of that supposedly comfortable place in the countryside dawned upon the inhabitants. From then on, it became more and more difficult to fill the steadily increasing quota the SS demanded from Lodz. People tried to hide among relatives and friends. Those in hiding got no food. After a while, their relatives were also denied food. Extreme altruism was shown. When people were found, other family members – still able to work – would often refuse the privilege of staying in Lodz, and instead joined children, the sick, or parents on what they by now knew was their last journey. The police, the Jewish police, had an increasingly difficult job in detecting, arresting, and deporting all those who tried to hide, but it had to be done, if the ghetto was to survive. As a reward to the policemen, their close relatives were exempt from deportation, until, in the end, they were all sent. Rumkowski himself, and his young wife, seem to have been deported in one of the last trains out of Lodz. A newspaper came out each day in the life of the ghetto, in four copies, for the inner circle. One was pre-served, and large parts are now available in an English edition (Dobroszycki 1984). Not many documents can have been published more naked in the description of the largeness of humans than this one. Nor can there be many such documents showing the other side of humanity: the possibility of total destruction under duress, when hunger, humidity, frost, and desperation destroyed everything, or where otherwise decent people lost all usual inhibitions in attempts to rescue their loved ones from deportation.

So, as we all know from our personal life, there are no absolute guarantees in that common core based on similar early experience. Often it works, in relation to those we are close to. But the core can be made irrelevant by distance, or by the extreme character of the surroundings one lives in.

Or it can be made irrelevant by professional training and practice.

This is not the place to denounce professionalism. It is a blessing to be at the receiving end of high quality professional service when that service is what we have asked for and we know we need. But a dilemma is inevitable. Professional training means long specialization. It means a purification of certain skills, but also of certain values. Long specialization means long distance from the basic core of human experience. Professionalization most often means a guarantee of a good job done in the area concerned, but reduced guarantees of attention to the totality of values, to the popular common sense. What happened to medicine in Nazi times is not so peculiar. There are no built-in guarantees.

Against this background, we may again turn our attention to law. That profession works with values. If lawyers can't be trusted, who can?

That depends on what sort of law.

It depends, first and foremost, on how close that law is to the core of common human experience. Will it be a law with roots in these core areas, or will it be a law alienated from that area, and instead completely anchored in the needs of the nation, in the needs of the government, or in the general management of the industrial/economic establishment? Or, in a formulation suggesting what I believe is the ideal: how can one achieve the highest legal standards in all these special fields, without losing sight of the core norms and values drawn from the well of common human experience?

13.2 Where does law belong?

Dag Østerberg (1991) divides the major social institutions in society into four basic categories. One is for production, where rational goal attainment is predominant. Another is for reproductive institutions, where caring and service dominate. In a third category, we find the institutions of politics and power, and in a fourth the institutions for coordinating principles, values and ways of thinking. This last category is where cultural and scientific institutions belong, where knowledge is produced and reproduced, where the everlasting discussion takes place on how the world is to be perceived, and on the relationship between nature and humans.

And where does law belong? Hedda Giertsen (1991) discusses this problem in a paper with the title "Law as humanistic activity". Her answer is reflected in the title. Rather than considering law as belonging to power and politics, she points to the essentially humanistic aspects of taking decisions on legal questions. Law has to do with conceptualization and evaluation, works with often conflicting phenomena, and is not limited to dealing with exact weights on a one-dimensional scale.

With modernity, all this has changed. Law has been pushed in the direction of the first general class of institutions, that of production. Law is becoming an instrument of utility, removed from its proximity to the cultural institutions. Through that move, law loses essential qualities, particularly its roots in the core area of human experience.

The classification of the total set of institutions into four basic types makes it possible to see the problems of integrating elements from one major type of institution into institutions belonging to the other basic categories. Solutions in one class of institution are not necessarily suitable in other types. Universities cannot be run as factories (even though some chancellors try to) without some loss of imaginative and critical ability. Likewise, courts cannot function as instrumental tools for management without sacrificing their greatest strengths in the protection of values: spelling them out, evaluating them against each other, and also seeing to it that single-minded goals in some institutional settings are not given undue weight in the totality. Law as a humanistic discipline keeps contact with the deep human activities, and thereby with the common experience. With that anchorage, the judiciary is prepared to meet the unbelievable, and react instinctively, as if in the family circle at the dinner table. There may be no law against executions in respirators, but it does not sound right, and it ought to be stopped.

I remember a guest from Poland who visited our institute many years ago. It was in the worst period of oppression in the East. Prison figures were steadily increasing from the very low level they were at before the Second World War. Figures were still not being censored, and we asked our guest, Dr. Jerzy Jasinski from the Polish Academy of Science, to explain the trend. He made no mystery of it.[5] The old judges were all gone. The new ones came from the party. But it was not necessarily party politics that were behind the newcomers' more severe sentencing. It had more to do with cultural affiliation. The old ones came from the intelligentsia; they belonged, which could rightly be criticized, to a sort of cultural élite. This probably meant a lot of snobbishness – I am afraid I am now leaving what Dr. Jasinski may have told us and going on with my own interpretations – but it also meant close contact with those Polish people who worked with the core problems of their time. It also meant close contact with people who in their personal life-styles would tend to expose tendencies and dilemmas which would be kept under cover in circles closer to the centre of power. A judge solidly based in the cultural arena both in reading and in life would not so easily be trapped into the belief that those he sentenced were of a completely different breed.

Common ground across social classes can be established through recruitment from all those classes. Matters can be arranged so that judges come from all social classes, with varied ethnic backgrounds representative of the country. The danger in the process is a loss of roots. The lower-class judge may become more upper-class in his identifications than anyone born there. The only viable alternative seems to be to preserve the common ground through a deep integration of law in culture. This would mean, in training as well as in practice, a heavy emphasis on the general principles of law, and discouragement of all sorts of specialization. It would also mean an encouragement to work with core values and norms, and greater ability to balance many

5 Later, in a more guarded form, the views were presented in The Polish Sociological Bulletin (Jasinski 1976).

values, many concerns and even many institutions, and not be carried away by fast simplistic solutions.

But such actions demand strength, and judges in armour. Arrogance is one such protection. That is the irony of the situation. The most democratically recruited judge, an equal among equals, might in an unequal society be badly equipped to show independent respect for the core values. In a society with gross inequalities, it seems to be particularly important to tie the judge as closely as possible to all those other workers on symbols, on meaning, on understanding and on further development of the common core.

Adherence to the common core also demands some freedom from other authorities. A judge reduced to a functionary pushing a button to produce the right answer is very far from free.

Penal law is a legal area in particular need of an independent judiciary based in culture.

13.3 A suitable amount of pain

We have seen that the level of imprisonment in society is not determined by crime, that punishment is not just a simple reaction to evil deeds, that it does not much affect the crime level where we place the punishment level, and that law is no natural instrument for management. This also sets us free from the burden of utility. Even to those who stick to utilitarian views of punishment, it becomes clear that there is a choice. To the rest of us, this has been clear all the way.

But this freedom immediately raises new problems. If punishment is not created by crime, how should we then determine the suitable amount of pain to be delivered within a particular society? We are free, but without clear guidelines. Why should we not have more people in prisons than we have at present? Why not a fifth of the male population, or a third for that matter? Why not re-introduce public flogging? And why not make extensive use of the death penalty?

It is possible to find an answer. It is possible, if we attempt to preserve the proximity between the institution of law and the other cultural institutions. A suitable amount of pain is not a question of utility, of crime control, of what works. It is a question of standards based on values. It is a cultural question.

There are two major ways of approaching this problem. One is to create penal theories based on strong unquestioned authorities. Utility theories have the State as their foundation. Most non-utility theories have scripts from God, prophets or other authorities. Their conception is one where the truth exists somewhere out there, given by absolute authority, and the task for the scholar is only to translate that truth into modern language. The non-utilitarian of this type is only a spokesman for God, exactly as the utilitarian is for the State. But even a cultural perspective can be captured by the state. Hitler himself decided on questions of art, particularly in painting and music. But other cultural expressions were also important to him. They expressed the state, and had to be decided by the state, which meant him. Franco, Mussolini and Stalin had similar inclinations.

An alternative to a conception of law as something existing, ready-made, from God or nature, is one where the basic principles of justice are there, all the time, but where the concrete formulations have to be re-created again and again. This alternative is one where justice does not consist of ready-made principles to be excavated using the methods applied in law or in the social sciences, but of common knowledge which each generation has to formulate into legal principles. This is a conception of each human being as a moral agent, and, to connect it to natural law, with each and every one of us as a prophet.

Punishment can then be seen to reflect our understanding and our values, and is therefore regulated by standards people apply every day for what is possible and what is not possible to do to others. These standards are in use, not just shown in opinion surveys. More than a tool for social engineering, the level and kind of punishment is a mirror of the standards that reign in a society. So the question for each and every one of us is: would it be in accordance with my general set of values to live in a state which represented me in this particular way? The National Theatre in Oslo represents me as a Norwegian. So do Henrik Ibsen and Edvard Grieg. But so does the fact that we executed

25 prisoners after the Second World War. The killing of Quisling is a part of me. So is the magnitude of our prison population which also in my country can be characterized as "An Affront to Civilized Society" (Stem 1987, pp. 1-8). But in belonging to Western industrialized culture, I am of course also represented by what happens in the USA. It is in a way also a part of me that cultural relatives find it acceptable to do such things to so many fellow citizens.

It is not obligatory to have a National Theatre, or money for artists. Arguments in favour can only be based on values. To me it is right to have them; terribly expensive, but right. The same is, ultimately, behind the critique of certain forms of punishment. It does not feel right to cut off fingers as a punishment, not any more. We felt it was acceptable up to 1815, when it was removed as a punishment from the penal code. To me it does not feel right to have 2,800 people in prison either. We are free to decide on the pain level we find acceptable. There are no guidelines, except in values.

Those of us who work close to penal systems have special responsibilities, but not as experts. As a criminologist I feel more and more that my function is very similar to that of a book reviewer or art critic. The script is not consistent, and can never be. The authors – the law committee in the Storting for example – are not in a position where they will ever be able to give a plausible description, in a law, of the totality of the problem they handle. A legal system without room for manoeuvre creates scripts and performances like those one meets in totalitarian régimes. Everything is predetermined, for the benefit of the rulers.

Rulers, and in democratic states, politicians, invariably attempt to give the impression that theirs are rational tasks in a field where utility thinking is of obvious importance. Our counter-idea as cultural workers – or members of the intelligentsia as they would say in Eastern Europe – is to puncture this myth and bring the whole operation back to the cultural arena. The delivery of pain, to whom, and for what, contains an endless line of deep moral questions. If there are any experts here, they are the philosophers. They are also often experts at saying that the problems are so complex that we cannot act. We must think. That may not be the worst alternative when the other option is delivery of pain.

Literature

Abel, P., B. Hebenton, T. Thomas, and S. Wright 1991 *The Technopolitics of Exclusion*. Unpublished paper prepared for the XIXth Annual Conference of the European Group for the Study of Deviance and Social Control. Potsdam, Germany, 4–8 September 1991.

Abramkin, Valery 1998 Criminal policy, retributive and restorative justice. *Human Beings and Prison.* Moscow Centre for Prison Reform, Moscow.

Adorno, T.W., Else Frenkel-Brunswik, Daniel Levinson, and R. Nevitt Sanford 1950 *The Authoritarian Personality*. Harper & Row, New York.

Andenæs, Johs 1991 Lovmotiver og strafferett. *Lov og Rett.* 1991, pp. 385–387.

Austin, James and Aaron David McVey 1989 *The 1989 NCCD Prison Population Forecast: The Impact of the War on Drugs.* The National Council on Crime and Delinquency, Washington.

Balvig, Flemming 1990 *Mod et nyt kriminologisk samfundsbillede.* (Towards a new Criminological Perspective on Society). Jurist- og økonomforbundets forlag, København.

Bauman, Zygmunt 1989 *Modernity and the Holocaust.* Polity Press, Cambridge.

Blumstein, Alfred 1991 Demographic Factors: Now and in the Future. *Growth and Its Influence on Correctional Policy.* Guggenheim Criminal Justice Program, Berkeley, USA.

Boyd, David G. 1994 *Virtual Dual Use: Doubling the Value of Defense Research and Development.* National Institute of Justice, Washington.

Bäckman, Johan 1998a *The Inflation of Crime in Russia. The Social Danger of the Emerging Markets.* National Research Institute of Legal Policy, Helsinki.

Bäckman, Johan 1998b *The Inflation of Crime in Russia.* Presentation at a seminar organized by Scandinavian Research Council for Criminology, Espoo, Finland 1998.

Bødal, Kåre 1982 *350 narkoselgere* (350 Drug Dealers). Universitetsforlaget, Oslo.

Christie, Nils 1952–53 *Fangevoktere i konsentrasjonsleire* (Guards in Concentration Camps). Articles 1952–53, book 1972.

Christie, Nils 1981 *Limits to Pain.* Universitetsforlaget, Oslo.

Christie, Nils 1987 Death and Crime. *Social problems and criminal justice.* 1987, pp. 19–31.

Christie, Nils 2000 A most usefull mafia. *Annual report from Institute of Criminology, University of Oslo.* Institute of Criminology, Oslo.

Cohen, Stanley 1985 *On Visions of Social Control.* Polity Press, Cambridge.

Cohen, Stanley 1992 *On Talking about Torture in Israel.* Manuscript.

Cooley, Charles H. 1956 *Social Organization: A Study of the Larger Mind.* First edition (1909), reprint (1956). Schocken books, New York.

Correctional Populations in the United States, 1996. Bureau of Justice Statistics Bulletin, U.S. Department of Justice, Washington April 1999.

Coyle, Andrew 2000 *Supermax Prisons: A New American Phenomenon.* Manuscript. International Centre for Prison Studies. Kings College. University of London.

Cunningham, William C., John J. Strauchs, and Clifford W. Van Meter 1991 *Private Security: Patterns and Trends.* National Institute of Justice: Research in Brief, August 1991.

Dahrendorf, Ralf 1985 *Law and Order.* The Hamlyn Lectures; 37. Stevens & Sons, London.

Dobroszycki, Lucjan 1984 *The Chronicle of the Lódz Ghetto 1941–1944.* Yale University Press, New Haven.

Downes, David 1988 *Contrasts in Tolerance. Post-War Penal Policy in The Netherlands and England and Wales.* Claredon Press, Oxford.

Durkheim, Émile 1966 *Suicide. A Study in Sociology.* Free Press, New York.

Ericson, Richard V., Maeve W. McMahon, and Donald G. Evans 1987 Punishing for Profit: Reflections on the Revival of Privatization in Corrections. *Canadian Journal of Criminology.* 1987, pp. 355–387.

Evans, Linda and Eve Goldberg 1999 *The Prison Industrial Complex and the Global Economy.* JusticeNet Prison Issues Desk. Prison Activist Resource Center, Berkeley.

Farmer, Paul 1998 *Cruel and Unusual: Drug-Resistant Tuberculosis as Punishment.* Department of Social Medicine (manuscript). Harvard Medical School.

Feeley, Malcolm M. 1991a *The Privatization of Prisons in Historical Perspective.* Criminal Justice Research Bulletin. Sam Houston State University. 1991, No. 2, pp. 1–10.

Feeley, Malcolm 1991b The New Penology. Reformulating Penal Objectives and Implications for Penal Growth. *Growth and Its Influience on Correctional Policy.* Guggenheim Criminal Justice Program, Berkeley.

Fellner, Jamie and Marc Mauer 1998 *Losing the vote. The impact of felony Disenfranchment Laws in the United States.* The Sentencing Project. Human Rights Watch.

Fridhov, Inger Marie 1988 *I all stillhet. En beretning om hvordan det oppleves å vente på bli satt i fengsel.* Mimeographed, Institute of Criminology, Oslo.

Garland, David 1986 The punitive mentality: Its socio-historic development and decline. *Contemporary Crises.* 1986, pp. 305–320.

Giddens, Anthony 1984 *The Constitution of Society. Outline of the theory of structuration.* Polity Press, Cambridge.

Giertsen, Hedda 1991 *On Giving Meaning to Murder.* Lecture to be published, University of Torino, May 1991.

Gusfield, Joseph R. 1963 *Symbolic Crusade. Status Politics and the American Temperance Movement.* University of Illinois Press, Urbana, Illinois.

Haan, Willem de 1991 Abolitionism and Crime Control: a Contradiction in Terms. In: Stenson, Kevin and David Cowell: *The Politics of Crime Control.* Sage, London.

Harris, Marvin 1981 *Why Nothing Works. The Anthropology of Daily Life.* Simon & Schuster, New York.

Hayes, Peter 1987 *Industry and Ideology. I.G.Farben in the Nazi Era.* Cambridge University Press, Cambridge.

Helsinki Watch (A Division of Human Rights Watch) 1991 *Prison Conditions in the Soviet Union. A Report of Facilities in Russia and Azerbaidzhan.* Helsinki Watch, New York.

Henry, Alan D. and John Clark 1999 *Pretrial Drug Testing: An Overview of Issues and Practices.* Bureau of Justice Assistance Bulletin. U.S. Department of Justice. Office of Justice Programs, Washington.

Hilberg, Raul 1985 *The Destruction of the European Jews.* Vol. I–III. Holmes & Meier, New York.

Home Office 1990 *Crime, Justice and Protecting the Public. The Government's Proposals for Legislation.* Cm 965. HMSO, London.

Hulsman, Louk 1974 Criminal Justice in the Netherlands. *Delta. A Review of Arts, Life and Thoughts in the Netherlands.* 1974, pp. 7–19.

Human Rights Watch 1992 *Prison Conditions in the United States.* Human Rights Watch, USA.

Human Rights Watch 1997 *Cold Storage. Super-Maximum Security Confinement in Indiana.* Human Rights Watch, USA.

Illich, Ivan 1971 *Deschooling Society.* Harper & Row, New York.

Illich, Ivan 1973 *Celebration of Awareness. A Call for Institutional Revolution.* Penguin Education, Harmondsworth.

Illich, Ivan 1974 *Energy and Equity.* Calder & Boyars, London.

Illich, Ivan 1976 *Limits to Medicine.* Marion Boyars, London.

Illich, Ivan 1978 *The Right to Useful Unemployment and Its Professional Enemies.* Marion Boyars, London.

Illich, Ivan 1982 *Gender.* Pantheon Books, New York.

Illich, Ivan 1992 Needs. *The Development Dictionary. A Guide to Knowledge and Power.* Sachs, Wolfgang (ed.). Zed Books, London.

Illich, Ivan and Barry Sanders 1988 *ABC: the Alphabetization of the Popular Mind.* North Point Press, San Fransisco.

Ingle, Joseph B. (with a Foreword by William Styron) 1990 *Last Rights. 13 Fatal Encounters with the State's Justice.* Abingdon Press, Nashville.

Jasinski, Jerzy 1976 The Punitiveness of the Criminal Justice System. *The Polish Sociological Bulletin.* 1976, pp. 43–51.

King, Roy D. 1994 Russian Prisons after Perestroika: End of the Gulag? *British Journal of Criminology.*1994, pp. 62–82.

Knepper, Paul and J. Robert Lilly: *The Corrections-Commercial Complex.* Paper presented at the Academy of Criminal Justice Sciences Conference, Nashville, Tennessee 1991.

Ladurie, Emmanuel Le Roy 1978 *Montaillou. Cathars and Catholics in a French Village 1294–1324.* Scholar Press, London. (In French: *Montaillou: village occitan de 1294–1324.* Éditions Gallimard, Paris 1975.)

Langan, Patrick A., and David P. Farrington 1998 *Crime and Justice in the United States and in England and Wales, 1981–96.* U.S. Department of Justice. Office of Justice Programs. Bureau of Justice Statistics, Washington.

Langbein, John H. 1978-79 Torture and Plea Bargaining. *The University of Chicago Law Review.* 1978–79, pp. 3–22.

Lapido, David 1999 *Regulating the American Labour Market. The Role of the Prison Industrial Complex. School of Sociology and Social Policy.* University of Nottingham. Paper presented at the 21st Conference of the International Working Party on Labour Market Segmentation, Bremen, Germany, 9–11 September, 1999.

Lea, John and Jock Young 1984 *What is to be Done about Law and Order?* Penguin Books, Harmonsworth.

Lifton, Robert Jay 1986 *The Nazi Doctors. Medical Killing and the Psychology of Genocide.* Macmillian, London.

Lindqvist, Sven 1992 *Utrota Varenda Jävel.* Bonniers, Stockholm.

Logan, Charles 1990 *Private Prisons. Cons and Pros.* Oxford University Press, New York.

Lotke, Eric 1996 The Prison-Industrial Complex. *Multinational Monitor.* November 1996, pp. 18–21.

Lång, K.J. 1989 Upplever fängelsesstraffet en renässans? Spekulationer om frihetsstraffets framtid. *Nordisk Tidsskrift for Kriminalvidenskab.* 1989, pp. 83–94.

Mann, Coramae Richey 1982 The Reality of a Racist Criminal Justice System. *Criminal Justice Research Bulletin.* No. 5, pp. 1–5.

Mathiesen, Thomas 1974 *The Politics of Abolition: Essays in Political Action Theory.* Scandinavian Studies in Criminology; 4. Scandinavian University Press, Oslo.

Mathiesen, Thomas 1990 *Prison on Trial. A Critical Assessment.* Sage, London.

Mauer, Marc 1991 *Americans Behind Bars: A Comparison of International Rates of Incarceration.* The Sentencing Project, Washington.

Mauer, Marc 1999 *Race to Incarcerate.* The Free Press, New York.

Mauer, Marc and Tracy Huling 1995 *Young Black Americans and the Criminal Justice System: Five Years Later.* The Sentencing Project, Washington.

Messinger, Sheldon and John Berecochea 1991 Don't Stay Too Long But Do Come Back Soon. Reflections on the Size and Vicissitudes of California's Prisoner Population. *Growth and Its Influence on Correctional Policy.* Guggenheim Criminal Justice Program, Berkeley.

Miller, Jerome G. 1996 *Search and Destroy. African-American Males in the Criminal Justice System.* Cambridge University Press, New York.

Mitford, Jessica 1974 *The American Prison Business.* Allen & Unwin, London. Published in the US. 1971 as *Kind and Usual Punishment.*

Morén, Kikki 1991 *Den europeiske festning? – Asylpolitikk og politisamarbeid mot 1992.* Institute of Criminology, Oslo.

Morrison, David C. 1994 Robocops. *National Journal.* 1994, pp. 889-893.

National Update January 1992. Bureau of Justice Statistics. National Update 1992 Vol. 1, No. 3. U.S. Department of Justice, Washington.

Nauke, Wolfgang 1982 Die Kriminalpolitik des Marburger Programms 1882. *Zeitschrift für die gesamte Strafrechtswissenschaft.* 1982, pp. 525–564.

Novak, Michael 1982 Mediating Institutions: The Communitarian Individual in America. *The Public Interest.* 1982, pp. 3–20.

Nozick, Robert 1974 *Anarchy, State and Utopia.* Basil Backwell, Oxford.

Palmær, Carsten and Ola 1986 *Vladmir Vysotskij. Sånger 1959–80*, p. 104. Ordfront, Stockholm.

Prisoners in 1998. Bureau of Justice Statistics Bulletin August 1999. U.S. Department of Justice, Washington.

Radzinowicz, Sir Leon 1991a Penal Regression. *The Cambridge Law Journal.* 1991, pp. 422–444.

Radzinowicz, Sir Leon 1991b *The Roots of the International Association of Criminal Law and their Significance.* Criminological Research Reports by the Max Planck Institute for Foreign and International Penal Law, Freiburg, Germany, Vol. 45, 1991.

Radzinowicz, Sir Leon, and Roger Hood 1981 The American volte-face in sentencing thought and practice. *Crime, Proof and Punishment. Essays in Memory of Sir Rupert Cross.* Tapper, C.F. (ed.). Butterworths, London.

Ratusjinskaja, Irina 1988 *Grey is the Colour of Hope* (Seryj svet nadezdy). In Norwegian 1988. Cappelen, Oslo.

Rawlinson, Patricia 1998 Mafia, Media and Myth. *The Howard Journal.* 1998, No. 43, pp. 46–358.

Rawls, John 1973 *A Theory of Justice.* Oxford University Press, Oxford.

Reno, Janet 1993 Opening Address at conference on "Law Enforcement Technology for 21st Century." *First presented at John Hopkins 1993 on a seminar on non-lethal Defence.*

Robert, Phillipe 1989 The Privatization of Social Control. *Crime and Criminal Policy in Europe.* Hood, Roger (ed.). Centre for Criminological Reseach, University of Oxford.

Rohn, Warren and Trish Ostroski 1991 Checking IDs. Advances in Technology Make it Easier to Monitor Inmates. *Corrections Today*, July 1991.

Rosenthal, Uriel and Bob Hoogenboom 1990 *Some Fundamental Questions on Privatisation and Commercialisation of Crime Control. With Special Reference to Developments in the Netherlands.* Collected Studies in Criminological Research, Vol. XXVII. Council of Europe, Strasbourg.

Rutherford, Andrew 1984 *Prisons and the Process of Justice. The Reductionist Challenge.* Heinemann, London.

Sachs, Wolfgang 1992 *The Development Dictionary. A Guide to Knowledge as Power*. Zed Books, London.

Scherdin, Lill 1990 *Sprøyten som språk. Injeksjonssprøyten i et kontrollpolitisk perspektiv*. Thesis. Institute of Criminology, University of Oslo.

Schlosser, Eric 1998 The Prison Industrial Complex. *The Atlantic Monthly*. 1998, No. 6, pp. 51–77.

Shearing, Clifford D., and Philip C. Stenning (eds.) 1987 *Private Policing*. Sage publications, Newbury Park.

Simmel, Georg 1950 The Metropolis and Mental Life, and The Stranger. *The Sociology of Georg Simmel*. Translated, edited and with an introduction by Kurt H. Wolf. The Free Press, Glencoe. Original edition: *Die Grosstadt*, Vorträge und Aufsätze zur Städteausstellung, Jahrbuch der Gehe-Stiftung 1903, 9, pp. 185–206 and Exkurs über den Fremden. Soziologie. Untersuchungen über die formen der Vergesellschaftung.

Smith, Albert G. 1991 Arming Officers Doesn't Have to Change an Agency's Mission. *Corrections Today*. 1991, No. 4, pp. 114–124.

Sorcebook of criminal justice statistics 1997. Bureau of Justice statistics. U.S. Department of Justice, Washington.

Spitzer, Steven 1974 Toward a Marxian Theory of Deviance. *Social Problems*, 1974, pp. 638–651.

Statistical Collection 1991 *Crimes and other offences in the USSR 1990*. Moscow.

Steenhuis, D.W., L.C.M. Tigges, and J.J.A. Essers 1983 The Penal Climate in the Netherlands. Sunny or Cloudy? *The British Journal of Criminology*. 1983, pp. 1–16.

Stern, Vivien 1987 *Bricks of Shame. Britain's Prisons*. Penguin, London.

Stern, Vivien 1999 The Cells of Death. The Tuberculosis Epidemic in the Prisons of the Former Soviet Union. *Prison Service Journal*. July 1999, pp. 2–4. A more complete coverage can be found in: Stern, Vivien (ed): *Sentenced to die? The problem of TB in prisons in Eastern Europe and Central Asia*. International Centre for Prison Studies, London.

Stimson, William A. 1991 A Better Design for Safer Detention on Death Row. *Corrections Today*. 1991, No. 4, pp. 158–159.

Swaaningen, René van, John Blad, and Reiner van Loon 1992 *A Decade of Research on Norm Production and Penal Control in the Netherlands*. Working documents of the centre for Integrated Penal Sciences, Erasmus University. Centre for Integrated Penal Sciences, Rotterdam.

The Corrections Yearbook. Instant Answers to Key Questions in Corrections 1991. Criminal Justice Institute, New York.

The Corrections Yearbook 1996 Camille Graham Camp and George Camp (eds.). Criminal Justice Institute, New York.

Tocqueville, Alexis 1990 *Democracy in America*. Vintage Books, New York.

Tonry, Michael 1991 The Politics and Processes of Sentencing Commissions. *Crime and Delinquency*. 1991, pp. 307–329.

Tørnudd, Patrik 1991 *15 years of Decreasing Prisoner Rates in Finland*. Mimeographed. The National Research Institute of Legal Policy.

United States Senencing Commission. Annual Report 1989. United States Senencing Commission, Washington.

United States Senencing Commission. Guidelines Manual 1990. United States Senencing Commission, Washington.

von Hirsch, Andrew 1976 *Doing Justice.* Report of the Committee for the study of incarceration. Hill and Wang, New York.

von Hirsch, Andrew 1982 Construction Guidelines for Sentencing: The Critical Choices for the Minnesota Sentencing Guidelines Commission. *Hamline Law Review.* 1982, pp. 164–215.

Wamsley, Roy 1999 *World Prison Population List.* Home Office Research, Development and Statistics Directorate. Research Findings No. 88. Home Office, London.

Weiss, Robert P. 1989 Private Prisons and the State. *Privatizing Criminal Justice.* Matthews, Roger (ed.). Sage Publications, London.

Wilbanks, William 1987 The Myth of a Racist Criminal Justice System. *Criminal Justice Research Bulletin.* 1987, No. 5, pp. 1–5.

Wolfgang, Marvin E., Arlene Kelly, and Hans C. Nolde 1962 Comparison of the Executed and the Commuted among Admissions to Death Row. *The Journal of Criminal Law, Criminology and Police Science.* 1962, No. 3, pp. 301–311.

Young, Jock 1989 Left Realism and the Priorities of Crime Control. *The Politics of Crime Control.* Stenson, Kevin and David Cowell (eds.). Sage, London.

Young, Jock and Roger Matthews (eds.) 1992 *Rethinking Criminology: The Realist Debate.* Sage, London.

Zimring, Franklin 1991 Correctional Growth in Context. *Growth and Its Influence on Correctional Policy.* Guggenheim Criminal Justice Program, Berkeley.

Østerberg, Dag 1991 Universitet og vitenskap i dagens samfunn. *Universitetets idé gjennom tidene og i dag.* Wyller, Egil A. (ed.). Universitetsforlaget, Oslo. Also in *Samtiden,* No. 3, 1991.